BUILD A BETTER
Toy Train Layout

John Grams &
Dick Christianson

KALMBACH
BOOKS

Acknowledgments

The collaborative effort that went into the LL/SF project at the outset was nothing short of phenomenal. We had friends and associates from both *Classic Toy Trains* and *Model Railroader* magazines enthusiastically coming over every Tuesday night, ready to pitch in for three hours or so.

Dick attributed this to what he called the "Tom Sawyer effect." The idea was to convince everybody that it was fun to build a model railroad (even more fun than whitewashing a fence).

If he could get the right people involved, and they worked as a team, the Tuesday night sessions would soon evolve into a social event, complete with smart talk, soda, and snacks. A little bragging and grandstanding would be all right as long as everyone could pool their skills – some might be better at carpentry, or wiring, or painting, or kit building, or scenery, or whatever – in a great utilization of collective talent.

As time went by, the guys were so pumped up by the project that one by one they decided to stay home on Tuesdays and build their own layouts. That's what can happen when the world's greatest hobby gets in your blood. (Well, one was an *NYPD Blue* fan.)

It took ten years of Tuesday nights to build the LL/SF. In the end, the only ones left were Huck and Tom.

©2004 Dick Christianson and John Grams
All rights reserved. This book may not be reproduced in part or in whole without written permission from the publisher, except in the case of brief quotations used in reviews. Published by Kalmbach Publishing Co., 21027 Crossroads Circle, Waukesha, WI 53187.

Printed in U.S.A.
04 05 06 07 08 09 10 11 12 13   10 9 8 7 6 5 4 3 2 1

Visit our website at http://kalmbachbooks.com
Secure online ordering available
ISBN 0-89778-479-0
Publisher's Cataloging-In-Publication Data
(Prepared by The Donohue Group, Inc.)

Grams, John.
  Build a better toy train layout / John Grams & Dick Christianson.

  p. ; cm.
ISBN: 0-89778-479-0

1. Railroads—Models. 2. Railroads—Models—Design and construction.
I. Christianson, Dick. II. Title.

TF197 .G73 2004
625.1/9

Art Director: Kristi Ludwig
Book design: Sabine Beaupré and Kory Beavers

Table of Contents

Introduction... **4**

1 – Planning the Layout: It's all in your head... **7**
By Dick Christianson

2 – Track Planning: Map your territory... **11**
By John Grams

3 – Benchwork: Built for the ages?... **17**
By Dick Christianson

4 – Trackwork: From the paper to the plywood... **23**
By John Grams

5 – Control/Wiring: ZW or TMCC or DCS?... **31**
By John Grams

6 – Scenery and Structures: Everyone can be an artist... **45**
By Dick Christianson

7 – Detailing: Where the fun really begins... **55**
By Dick Christianson

8 – Rolling Stock: It looks better when it's all the same height... **63**
By John Grams

9 – Maintenance: Keeping the good times rolling... **69**
By John Grams

10 – Operation: A brave new toy train world... **73**
By Dick Christianson

Suppliers... **80**

Introduction: Better than cousin Charlie's

By John Grams and Dick Christianson

As you probably noticed, the title of this book is *Build a Better Toy Train Layout*. We called it that because that was the subject of the book we wanted to write. The title implies that you've already built a layout and you're about to embark on another (or improve on the layout you already have).

Our aim is to help you build a better layout than your first one (or your second or third), a better layout than you thought you could build, a better layout than your cousin Charlie's, a better layout than you would have built without having read this book, or all of the above.

Do-it-yourself book

It is not our intent to tell you step by step how to build your next layout. Our goal is to equip you to build a better layout of your own design. We're going to provide you with some basic concepts about each aspect of layout building, give you some of the information you'll need (a lot of the details can be found in books we recommend), and show and tell you some of what we did to improve our layout.

In addition, we'll provide lists of questions to consider before you embark on each phase of layout building and some tips we think are important. Finally, we're going to share resources that have more detailed information than we have room for in this book.

You need to read

You'll discover that most of the books listed at the end of each chapter are scale model railroading books. Don't ignore them. They're loaded with good information, most of which applies to toy trains as well as to scale. After all, scenery is scenery; benchwork is benchwork; however, wiring is not wiring—that's why we didn't include any scale model wiring books in the list.

All the books listed are from Kalmbach Publishing Co., our publisher, and the number listed after each title is the number you can refer to when you call toll-free (1-800-533-6644) to order. Most of these books are also found in well-stocked hobby shops.

Who cares what we did?

The projects described in the book will be, we hope, interesting, entertaining, and informative. But maybe more important, we hope they will get you thinking.

We recognize that a specific mini-scene we built or the position of one of our tunnels won't necessarily be important to you. What we did may not even be possible (or desirable) to duplicate on your layout.

What will be important, though, is the thinking behind what we did and what we were trying to achieve.

You may also find that you don't want to do what we did, because what we did was, well, stupid. If you recognize what not to do, that in itself is a valuable lesson.

Our hope would be, though, that you can take one of our projects and improve upon it or modify it for your own layout. If you're able to do that, then the price you paid for the book will be worth it (the price is reasonable anyway!).

Maybe your layout is better already

As you page through this book, perhaps you'll realize that you've already built a layout that's "better" than ours. Great! If so, we still hope you'll enjoy some of the projects and can glean some ideas for your own layout—or your next one.

Please enjoy the thought process involved in building a better layout.

1

Planning the Layout: It's all in your head

By Dick Christianson

The title of this book promises that you can build a better toy train layout. Better than what? Better than the previous layout you built? Better than you thought you could? Better than someone else's layout? Yes, to all three.

There's really no trick to building a better layout. First, practice will improve your skills. Second, you've undoubtedly learned from the mistakes you made on your first layout (or layouts). Third, you've probably seen layouts in magazines or visited layouts that others have built and so you already have in mind ways you can improve your next layout.

To my mind, however, the key element in building a better layout is to think about it before you build it. In many ways, model railroading is an intellectual exercise. You think about the layout you'd like to have, you wonder where you can build it, and you ponder how big it should be. There seem to be more questions than answers!

You'll eventually need a hammer and saw. Layout building gets physical before too long. But much of the process takes place in your mind—before you even pick up a hammer or saw—or begin to plan with paper and pencil, for that matter. Building a layout requires you to think and to ask questions—and, ultimately, to answer those questions.

Remember the classic musical *The Music Man*? In it, Professor Harold Hill had the kids in his band "think" the music even before they had their instruments. Professional athletes these days "visualize" the outcome of their race or game. Supposedly that helps.

Well, I'm here to tell you that you will build a much better layout if you think about it first.

If you really want to build a better layout, resist the urge to start building, and worry about the details later.

I write from experience. Prior to starting the layout John and I built over the past 10 years, I decided to charge ahead like a bull in a china shop. Ah, the impetuousness of youth! My wife, daughters, and I had moved into a new home with a huge, empty, largely unfinished basement. The basement floors and walls were painted, but the ceiling was untouched. Only four or five bare light bulbs shed light on the entire space.

> *The key element in building a better layout is to think about it before you build it.*

Key layout planning questions

- Where will my layout be located?
- Should the layout be considered permanent or temporary?
- Will the layout room need work: light fixtures, carpeting, painting?
- Are there fixtures (furnace, water heater, couch, doors) that I'll need to work around?
- What is the actual size of the room?
- What will the layout's dimensions be?
- Will my layout be walkaround or be controlled from a panel?
- How much room do I need for aisles?
- What kind of equipment am I going to run?
- How skilled am I at benchwork, wiring, scenery, maintenance?
- How much money will I need to build my "better" layout?
- How much time do I have to build my "better" layout?

Most importantly, though, I knew I had half the basement on a permanent basis. So, unable to wait any longer, I put together a quick track plan and hurriedly built some L-girder benchwork.

Thankfully, before I'd gotten very far along I recognized that this was a mistake. I began to "visualize" myself on top of the benchwork, hanging a drop ceiling and putting in fluorescent light fixtures. Bad vision.

So, I stopped construction and began to think seriously about the layout I wanted to see when it was finished. The layout I saw in my mind had a carpeted floor beneath it, finished walls with shelving surrounding it, and a drop ceiling with fluorescent lights above it. That was a more pleasing vision. I tore down the benchwork and started planning the layout that would fit in the railroad room I envisioned.

To help you get started on your "visualizations," I've provided you with some questions you ought to ask yourself before you set out to build a better layout along with a few considerations I think might be helpful. In fact, this is the first step in that process.

Space considerations

Do you have a permanent location available? Or is it only on loan? Is the room eventually going to be a guest room? A nursery? A bedroom for a returning adult offspring?

Should the layout be permanent or portable? If you can anchor the layout to the walls or have no concern about having to move it, you can build a layout that has an air of permanency about it. However, if you're living in an apartment and could move at some point, you may want to make the layout sectional or small enough to move it to the next location. Be sure in this case to measure the doors and hallways before you build.

What are the physical attributes of the space? Do you have plenty of light? Does the room have enough outlets? Are there windows or doors to work around? Is the room finished or do you need to do that first? Do you care if the room is finished? What is the shape of the space? Are there furnaces or water heaters to work around?

How big or small is the room? Is the available space large enough to hold the layout you envision? What kind of operation will it allow? What about circles? Or can you build peninsulas and aisles to walk in to follow your train?

Personal preferences

Do you want to build a walkaround layout, or do you prefer to sit at a control panel and run the trains from there? Do you like to operate the trains like the real thing, or do you just enjoy watching them run? Do you want to run the operation by yourself, or do you expect to invite others to share in the fun?

Equipment available

Do you have a lot of leftover postwar Lionel trains and lots of track? Do you have only a little bit of equipment and want to start over with new trains and power sources? Are the trains you have in good enough shape to run reliably? Are you planning to replace your old trains with newer, more to-scale trains?

Do you have small locomotives that look okay on tight curves, or can your track plan have broad curves that will handle bigger locomotives and long passenger cars? Do you have accessories that you want to include and need to allow space for?

Skill level

Here's where you have to be honest with yourself. What kind of layout can you really build? Are your carpentry, electrical, and scenery skills currently at the level that will allow you to build your dream layout?

I knew my limitations when I started building. I could do the benchwork, tracklaying, and scenery, but wiring would be a challenge. That's why I was so pleased that John was willing and able to build the layout with me—and to share in the writing of this book. He's terrific at tracklaying, wiring, and maintenance.

Skill level. Here's where you have to be honest with yourself.

Layout planning resources

Great Toy Train Layouts by Roger Carp (10-8325)
Track Planning for Realistic Operation (3rd edition) by John Armstrong (12148)

If you can't do everything yourself, plan on finding a friend or reading a lot. Either way works, but it's sure nice to have another person to share the work and the fun.

Financial resources

Here's another gut-check point. Toy trains aren't exactly inexpensive. Neither is wood. So, if you're in a hurry to get a layout up and running, you need to ask: "What can I afford?" If, on the other hand, you see this as a long-term project, then the pressure's off. You can spread the costs over 2, 5, 10, or more years.

From the point John, some helpers, and I started on the LL/SF layout, it took just over 10 years to "complete." My wallet wouldn't have been able to support building a layout in 1 or 2 years, but over 10 years the budget worked out pretty well.

Think about this: if you golf, you may spend at least $20 every time you play. Let's say you play 15 times in a season—that's $300. Do that for 10 years and you've spent $3,000. You can build a pretty credible layout for that kind of money. So, figure the cost into the layout you have in mind.

Keep asking questions

Those are not all the aspects you should take into account before building your layout, but they'll get you started. I recommend that you write down random questions that come to mind about the layout. Categorize these areas of confusion—layout room, benchwork, wiring, rolling stock, and so forth—and then begin addressing them.

Decisions you make about early aspects of layout building will predetermine later issues. For example, having only a 10 x 12-foot space for your layout will mean it will not be able to accomodate long straightaway running. It may also mean that you won't be running scale-length passenger cars. And it can eliminate the need for digital command control because the entire layout will be within easy reach of the control panel.

With a good understanding of what you have to work with—space, equipment, skills, hobby preferences, and finances—you can get down to really planning your railroad.

Layout planning tips

- Spend plenty of time thinking about the layout you want to build—before you spend money on it.
- Ask yourself the key questions posed in this book and any others you think of. More importantly, answer them.
- Don't build your layout until you've considered every angle and imagined every eventuality.
- Don't be surprised when you start to build if you find angles you didn't consider and eventualities you didn't imagine.
- "Visualize" the layout you want and the space it will be in.

2

Track Planning: Map your territory

By John Grams

Once you have the available space measured down to the last inch, make a scale drawing of it. One inch = one foot is a popular ratio for small- to medium-sized spreads. One-half inch = one foot will work well for larger layout spaces. Anything smaller makes it difficult to draw a plan accurately—unless you're an expert draftsman with professional equipment.

Using cardstock templates to create a track plan on the floor made the benchwork easier to visualize before building. Sketching the plan with chalk on the basement floor also works.

Planning to build your layout in manageable steps is practical. You can modify the plan as you go along.

Be sure to measure and include in your scale drawing the size and location of all fixed obstacles that will affect your plan, such as windows, doors, pipes, drains, columns, tanks, water heater, and furnace. Bear in mind that some of these things may need service or replacement in the future, so don't box them in.

A number of aids on the market can help you draw a competent track plan. If you are working in 1 inch = 1 foot scale, look for plastic templates and cutout track sections.

If you are familiar with computer software, commercial track-planning programs are available. Check with your local hobby shop, or look for ads in *Classic Toy Trains* magazine.

The least expensive and most-often-used method is also the simplest—Bristol board and tracing paper. Make a scale outline of your available space in ink on the Bristol board. Lay a sheet of tracing paper over it, and fix the paper in place with masking tape at each corner.

You don't need a T-square, triangle or anything fancy. However, you may find good use for a three-sided architect's scale, a quality straightedge, a compass for drawing circles, medium pencils, and a soft eraser.

The tracing-paper method lets you move things around to see what will fit and what won't. If you make a mistake, tape on a fresh sheet of paper and try again. It's easier than drawing a new outline of the layout space each time you change your mind. And you *will* change your mind.

Planning to build your layout in manageable steps is practical. The tracing-paper method gives you a concrete visualization of the layout in all its stages.

It's important to start with a good track plan. That doesn't mean you have to stick to it slavishly. You can modify the plan as you go along—some trial and error is normal.

Choosing the kind of layout you want

In addition to the limits of available space, the type of layout you design will depend on the kind of railroad operation you enjoy most and, to some extent, on the nature of the rolling stock you intend to run on it.

Although the variations are infinite, there are essentially three types of layout designs:
- Continuous run
- Point-to-point

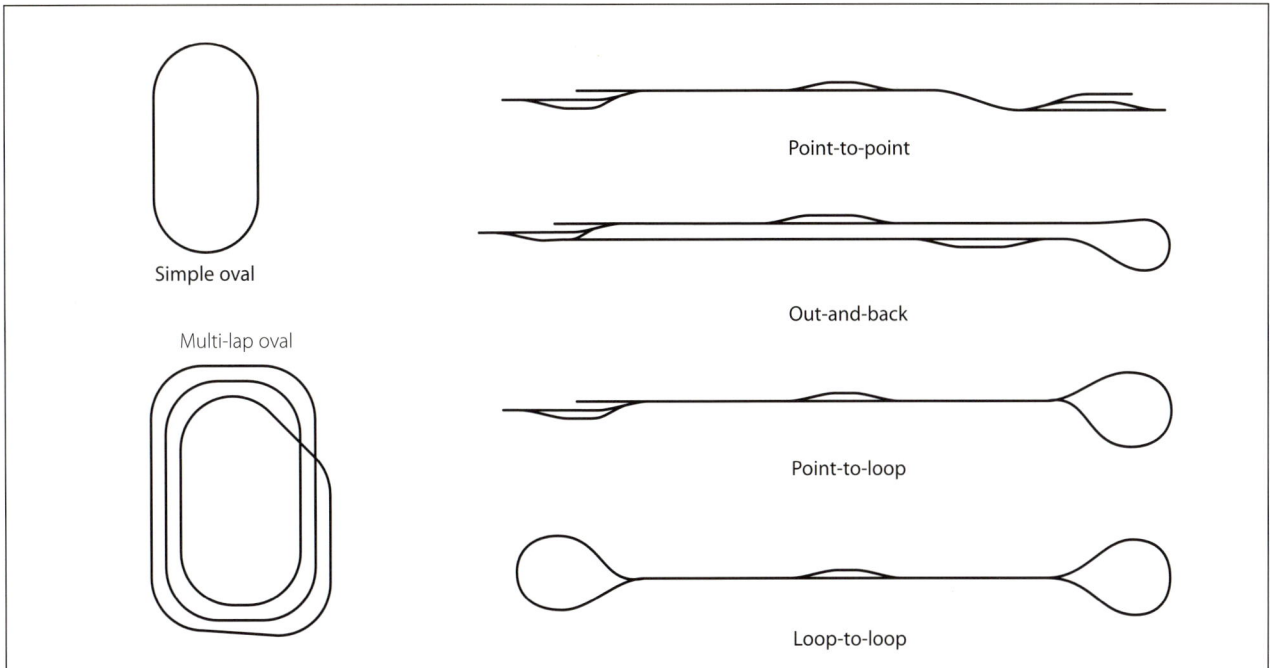

• A combination of the first two.

All can have provisions for a train to change direction, pass another train, and spot cars on sidings, but that doesn't change the basic types.

Continuous run. This arrangement allows a train to run over the entire layout continuously without the attention of the operator. This common plan runs the gamut from simple ovals to multiple-lap affairs.

Point-to-point. This type of layout most closely resembles prototype railroad practice. Real trains run from one point to another. Operation in this instance becomes an intensive, hands-on job that often requires the skill and coordination of several operators.

Combination. This kind of layout is by far the most popular. It combines elements from continuous run and point-to-point designs. There are three notable variations:
• Out and back
• Point and loop
• Loop to loop.

A central theme for your layout

Chances are that your available space doesn't represent much real-world acreage, even if you have an entire basement or attic at your disposal. You won't be able to model an entire railroad line, no matter how short it might be.

Most model railroaders focus on a single theme, locale, or type of activity that they enjoy most. Then they design their layout around it. Again, there are three general categories:

> ## Key track planning questions
> • Is the space-plan I've drawn accurate? Does it account for all the fixed obstacles?
> • Do I want to do a pencil-drawn layout with a template or use a computer program?
> • What kind of operation appeals to me: continuous run, point-to-point, or a combination?
> • Does the layout I visualize have a theme or focus?
> • Will I be the only person running the trains? Do I need to provide for more operators?
> • Will I be able to reach everything without having to climb on the layout?
> • If I can't reach everything, will I be able to add a pop-up or liftout section?
> • Do I want grades on the layout? Can I live with a couple of levels to suggest mountains?
> • Do I know the tricks that scale modelers have developed to make their plans interesting?
> • Should the layout have a backdrop or scenic divider to break up the scenes? Would I rather see everything at one time?

No wider than you can reach!

Never build a layout you have to climb on. As far as I'm concerned, this is an inviolable rule—the 11th Commandment that Moses forgot to tell us about.

If your plan calls for an area that's going to be out of arm's reach, scrap the plan and start over! Don't rationalize and talk yourself into it. If you have someone working with you, make them swear that they'll lock you away until you come back to your senses.

Here's why I'm so adamant about this. John and I started with a plan that's fairly close to the finished layout. We particularly liked the way it flowed through 72-inch-diameter curves—big sweeping S-curves that make streamlined passenger cars look good. Neither of us had had the space or opportunity to build layouts like this before.

Oh, there were going to be some spots that would be tough to reach, but installing backdrops down the center of the loops meant that we'd never have to reach farther than 36 inches. Pretty good in theory; not so good in practice.

As John and I began to build the layout, we succumbed to temptation. "If we widen the layout here we can get two or three more tracks in the yard," he said to me.

"Yeah, you're right. That would be pretty neat."

I knew that in the future I'd need to get up on the layout to lay track, solder feeders, put in extra ties, ballast the rails, rerail cars that always derail in the worst places. But that would be sometime in the future – not worth worrying about at the moment.

Here's the upshot of the story. I spent way too many long, painful evenings on my hands and knees doing those things. Take my advice! Unless you're 20 years old or have a high threshold of pain, don't design a layout you'll have to climb on. It ain't worth it!—*Dick Christianson*

- The open road
- Station operations
- Yards and/or industrial service.

Builders of small layouts will do well to focus on one of these. Those hobbyists with space for larger spreads may have the luxury of combining elements from two or all three.

The open road. This kind of operation is possible on larger layouts, where trains can open up while running through the countryside over wide-radius curves. The results are enjoyable and exciting, particularly when you're running sleek passenger trains or transcontinental freights.

Station operations. This works well with medium-sized layouts. Trains arrive and depart according to schedule, picking up and dropping off cars at the station. Successful operation demands quick wits because traffic has to be directed and problems solved as they arise.

Yards and/or industrial service. This is a favorite among operators who want to cram a lot of action into a small space. Model railroads that follow this theme tend to be switching layouts. Operators spot empty cars on industrial sidings as they pick up loaded ones. They assemble trains in yards, waiting for a road engine to take them away. The process can keep you pleasantly occupied for hours.

How many operators?

The number of operators you envision to run the layout is a serious consideration. Do you plan to handle everything yourself? A club? With a layout of any size and complexity, provisions should be made for multiple operators, at least on some occasions.

For example, the LL/SF functions with only one operator, but it's probably at its best with two of us stationed at the two main control positions. However, functions can be switched so that one person can handle most of it from either position. We can use three or four operators by dividing the labor and assigning specific sections.

Making it all fit

Ideally, everything should be within arm's reach in case something goes wrong. That is somewhere between 3 and 4 feet from the edge, depending on the length of your arms.

If that isn't possible, you should incorporate access spaces or hatches into the plan to accommodate human intervention when necessary. Otherwise, you'll wind up getting on top of the layout whenever something goes wrong in a hard-to-reach place. This may not be the worst thing, but it gets harder to do as the years take their toll.

Strive for the maximum utilization of

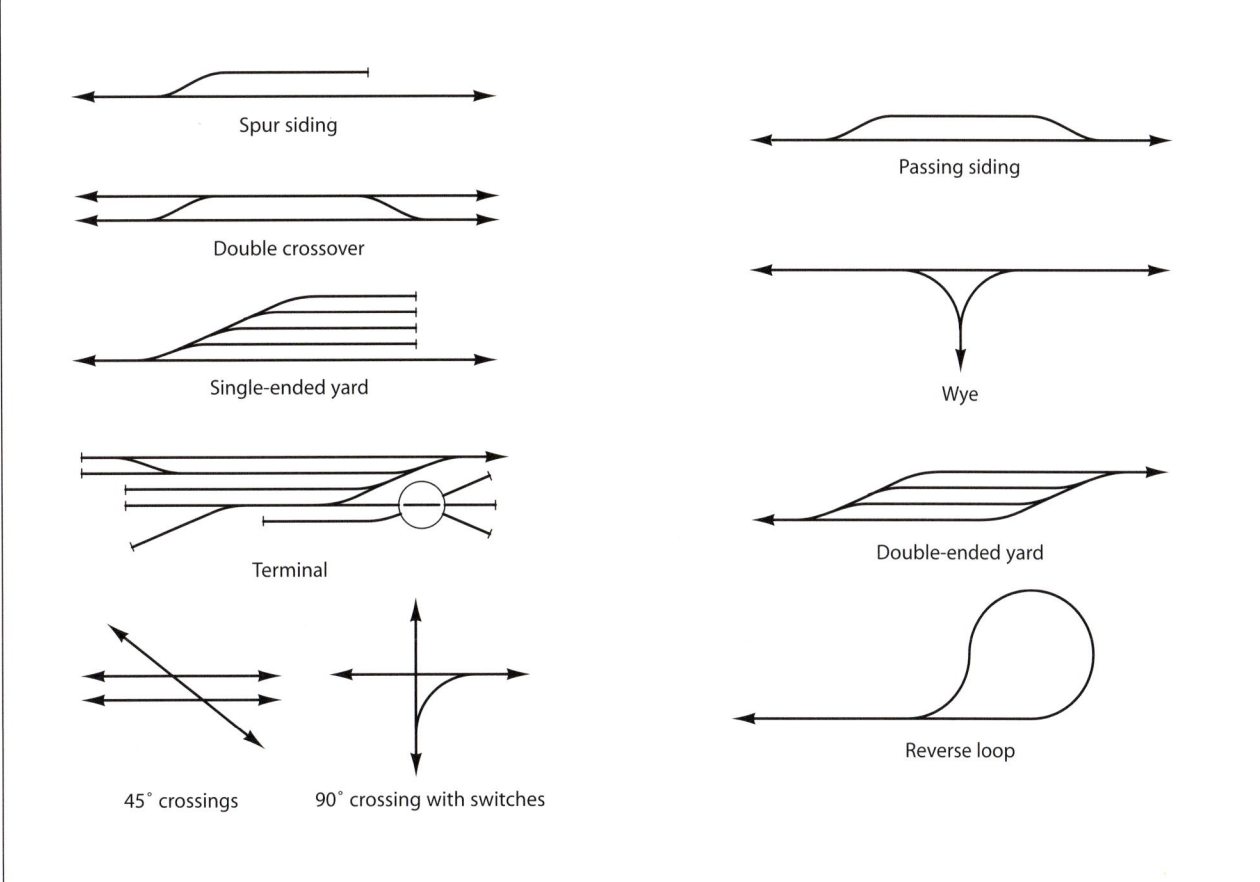

available space. This doesn't necessarily mean that every square foot has track running through it—though it could. It's your layout, so it's up to you.

Every track should have a purpose, a reason for being there (or at least it should look as though it does). By following real railroad practice in laying out track formations, you can do much to create this impression. Here are some of the more common ones:

- Spur siding
- Passing siding
- Crossover
- Wye
- Single-ended yard
- Double-ended yard
- Terminal
- Reverse loop
- Crossing

Hills to climb?

To have grades, or not to have grades? Operators have debated this for years with excellent arguments on both sides. It boils down to personal preference, along with the nature of the locale being modeled.

Having trains appear at different levels or elevations can be pleasing for viewers, but grades inevitably cause operational problems that can outweigh such considerations and detract from the fun of running the trains. That's why we chose to have two levels on the LL/SF, but with no connection or grades between them.

Track planning tips

- There is no substitute for a carefully laid out and measured scale track plan. Your plan can be modified slightly as you go along if it was initially sound and functional.
- Building your layout in steps or stages can be advantageous.
- The type of operation you want will determine the kind of layout you build.
- Strive for maximum utilization of available space.
- Every track should have a purpose.
- Borrow layout design ideas and techniques from scale model railroaders.

Thinking outside the box

Or rectangular plywood sheet, if you will.

Toy train enthusiasts tend to design track plans like the ones printed in old Lionel catalogs. Those plans featured 90- or 180-degree turns and track running parallel to the edge of the layout—visually interesting patterns that had no discernable purpose.

Emphasis was placed on geometry and balance, to the exclusion of real railroad practices. There's more potential for realism and operational satisfaction than that.

Don't be afraid to use scale layout design techniques and practices. Feel free to borrow ideas from hard-core "model railroader" types—they have lots to teach us.

Borrowing ideas and techniques from scale model railroaders is more obviously manifested in the scenery department (landscapes, buildings, and set dressings) but it all starts with a track plan that dictates the scenes themselves. There's no way that a typical, predictable, symmetrical toy train layout can look realistic, regardless of how good the scenic details might be.

Tracks shouldn't always run in a straight line along the edge of the benchwork and turn abruptly when the tabletop ends. In a good layout, one that tries to look natural, the benchwork is rarely linear, because there are few straight lines, right angles, and figure-eights in nature.

Sometimes it makes sense to place scenic details between the edge of the benchwork and the track to trick the eye. I've even seen some sweeping diagonals that work well within the context of a layout.

Backdrops and dividers

Scale model railroaders understand the value of backdrops in creating a credible scene and use them to give the illusion of depth and distance. Traditionally, backdrops are made of Masonite painted sky blue that extends above normal eye level. These usually feature pasted or painted scenery in perspective with three-dimensional objects in front of them leading into the picture. This technique is very effective, if done well.

Dividers are similar to backdrops in every way, but they also compartmentalize the layout into separate scenes when it's viewed from different angles or sides. The rules of backdrops also apply to dividers.

We made generous use of backdrops and dividers on the LL/SF, sometimes to the consternation of guest operators who were used to following the progress of their trains along the entire layout. Every scene on the layout has a backdrop.

On the lower level, one large divider separates the southern yards and oil plant from the northern locomotive-servicing facility, industries, and passenger terminal. The upper level crosses the dividers and backdrops several times. It is all very mysterious and fascinating, with wall-to-wall illusion.

Backstage is a different matter. There one finds unpainted plywood, Masonite, 1 x 2s, bare tracks, and wires—the naked truth that beauty is indeed only skin deep. Nobody is supposed to look there anyway.

I'm reminded of the out-of-town consultant who comes to your business sparkling with glitz and enthusiasm, in a rented Lexus, a $900 suit—and cheap underwear. He doesn't spend money on anything that doesn't show.

There's a lesson in there someplace.

Grades inevitably cause operational problems.

> **Track planning resources**
>
> *Classic Lionel Display Layouts You Can Build* by Roger Carp (10-8255)
> *Great Toy Train Layouts* by Roger Carp (10-8325)
> *Layout Plans for Toy Trains* by Kent Johnson (10-8275)
> *Mid-Sized & Manageable Track Plans* by Iain Rice (12245)
> *Realistic Model Railroad Design* by Tony Koester (12250)
> *Realistic Track Plans for O Gauge Trains* by Martin McGuirk (10-8215)
> *Track Planning for Realistic Operation* by John Armstrong (12148)
> *Track Planning Ideas for Toy Trains* by Peter Riddle (10-8310)
> *Track Plans for Toy Trains* by Kent Johnson (10-8230)

3

Benchwork: Built for the ages?

By Dick Christianson

A better layout should have better benchwork.
"Better benchwork? What's that all about?" "What difference does benchwork make? And what makes one kind better than another?" "*Kinds* of benchwork . . . there's more than one kind? Isn't benchwork just, well, benchwork?"

Good questions. The fact is, there are different types of benchwork, and the kind you choose for your railroad does matter.

Here's a rule of thumb: A simple layout doesn't need complex, sophisticated benchwork. Conversely, a complex layout needs more than simple benchwork.

Stability matters

Better benchwork—no matter which variety—has one primary characteristic: it's stable. The first layout my dad built for me when I was 5 or 6 was a flat sheet of 5 x 9 plywood. To the underside Dad attached threaded pipe brackets, one set in 12 inches or so from each corner and one in the center. Threaded into all five of these were steel pipes.

This arrangement was functional and adequate—but unstable. My layout wobbled a little like Jell-O whenever I bumped it. The wobble was not enough to cause the trains to fall off the tracks, but it was disconcerting nevertheless.

That experience was in my mind over the years as I built two N scale railroads and a couple of toy train layouts. I used scrap lumber for benchwork—leftovers from remodeling projects or the construction of our house. Most often the leftovers were 2 x 4s.

The benchwork beneath those layouts brings to mind what the building inspector said when he approved my overly substantial deck: "That will stand for a millennium!" Benchwork doesn't need to stand for a millennium or be able to survive a hurricane or tornado. It needs to support a layout, and sometimes the builder, without wobbling much.

Start by thinking about the layout you want to build. Think about what it needs to support it. Does the shape or location dictate the type of benchwork? Does the style (i.e., flattop, up and down grades) influence your selection of foundation?

Almost any support will work for a flattop layout: open grid, L girder, bookshelves, spare tables. Layouts with grades generally call for L girder or open grid. Get your hands on the recommended reading materials, and figure out what you'll need. The planning you did in the last chapter will guide your selection.

Narrowing choices

If you've followed our advice about asking and answering basic questions, you'll recognize that your choice of benchwork will at this point be almost automatic. For example, let's say you decide to build an around-the-walls layout in your family room. Benchwork made of 2 x 4s probably isn't necessary. You're never going to have to climb on the 12-inch-wide shelves on which your layout runs.

Some sort of cantilevered benchwork might be appropriate; even metal bookshelf brackets could work. Maybe a shelf suspended from the ceiling? How about bookshelves or cabinets supporting at least parts of the railroad? Think about the shape and position of your railroad.

How about a traditional layout in the center of the room with your collection displayed on shelves around the walls? If the layout is going to be flat and take up most of the central area, you're probably going to

---

Benchwork tips

- Benchwork needs to be stable and level.
- If your track plan allows track more than 3 feet from the edge, build in pop-up or liftout sections.
- You have many choices when it comes to benchwork. Think about the kind that will best suit the layout's needs and yours.
- L-girder benchwork is strong, stable, and economical in its use of wood. It's also flexible in the ways it can be used.
- An eye-level layout is neat, but don't build it so high that you can't see what's going on in back.
- A low-level layout allows you to view it as though you're in an airplane, but it's a back-breaker to work on.
- Build a layout to a height that's just right for you.
- Pick a subroadbed that deadens sound. The trains make plenty of noise, and, pleasant though that may be for awhile, it eventually gets grating.

Ties and ballast make all the difference

Dick and I are both traditionalists, determined to use classic Lionel tubular track on most of the layout and make the best of it. I'm not a bit sorry. In fact, I'm convinced that toy trains of any age run better on good old tinplated steel rails. It's part of the natural order of things. Of course, adding extra ties and realistic ballast to the roadbed can greatly enhance the realism of the layout.

The ties should be of the approximate size and shape of the sheet-metal ones built into the track sections. Yes, they're too large and out of scale, but using added ties in this configuration is more convincing than trying to put O scale ties next to the larger integrated ones.

Ties of this correct contour are available commercially in wood or plastic from several sources. Check with your local hobby shop or consult the ads in *Classic Toy Trains* magazine.

If you have a table saw, you can make your own ties quite inexpensively. That's the route Dick and I chose. Actually, Dick's dad cut most of them years ago for a layout that never got off the drawing board. Their dimensions match Lionel O gauge ties precisely—2" long, 5/8" wide and 3/16" high.

To imitate the aged creosote color of the prototypes, we mixed together several dark wood stains (whatever Dick had on his shelf), added mineral spirits, and dumped the ties into a bucket. After soaking them for about an hour, we fished out the ties and lined them up on a framed screen to drip-dry over a bed of newspaper. It took several days, but the results were excellent.

Appropriately sized ballast is available from a number of manufacturers in a variety of colors, ranging from gray to black, reflecting variations in the real thing. Ballast on the high iron is usually lighter than that found in yards and service areas, which is sometimes almost black. You can blend it to achieve great results.

Much of the commercial ballast these days is made of ground rubber, so it's light and easy to use. I know some

Ties and ballast have been added to standard tubular track. This ballast is black to represent the cinders often used in railroad yards and lightly used sidings. The mainline ballast is a light gray with some black mixed in to suggest shadows. A solid gray looks too neat and artificial.

modelers use bird gravel or cat litter because it's cheaper, but we saved enough money on the ties so we could splurge on the ballast.

With your fingers, work the ballast into a raised roadbed alongside and between the ties. Smooth it out at a level slightly below the tops of the ties. Be sure you get all, or nearly all, of the ballast pieces off the ties.

As a fixative, prepare a mixture of about 3 parts water to 1 part white glue. Add a few drops of liquid dish detergent to the solution to act as a wetting agent. With a household turkey baster, dispense a few drops between each tie. It will run down and dry solidly in place in a day or so.

Be careful around switches and switch machines. You don't want to get the innards wet and the contacts coated with glue. Clean the rails with a ScotchBrite pad when you're finished.—*John Grams*

The new three-rail systems compensate for this and match the detail of the new rolling stock by incorporating realistically spaced, scale-sized plastic ties. Great if you want to go that route; however, I think we have shown on the LL/SF that conventional sectional track can be made presentable by adding more ties of an appropriate size and color before ballasting. Making ties to match the integrated ones is more convincing than trying to put thin O scale ties between the larger metal ones.

Ties of this contour are available commercially in wood, rubber, or plastic from several sources. Check with your local hobby shop for particulars.

If you have a table saw, you can make your own ties quite inexpensively. The dimensions to match Lionel O gauge ties precisely are: 2¼" long, ⅝" wide, and 3/16" high. Once you have the saw set, you can probably turn out enough ties for your entire layout in an evening or two.

To simulate the aged creosote color of prototype ties, you can paint them in a dark gray flat color or do as we did. Dick had a few half-empty cans of different dark wood stains sitting on his shelf. We mixed them together in a bucket and added mineral spirits until the brew had the consistency of skim milk. [Note: Health issues are involved with solvent-based stains. Avoid getting stain on your hands. Work with the stuff outdoors. And let it dry outdoors or in the garage—anywhere where humans won't be breathing the fumes.]

Dick and I dumped the ties into the bucket and let them soak. In the meantime, we stretched vinyl window screen over a frame of 1 x 2s to serve as a drying rack.

After letting the ties soak for 30 minutes or so, we fished them out of the bucket and lined them up on the screen to drip-dry over several days. Of course, we had placed the screen over several layers of newspaper to catch the drippings. We put them in the garage to dry.

A rocky finish

Appropriately sized ballast is available from a number of manufacturers and suppliers in a variety of colors ranging from light gray to black to reflect color variations in the real thing. Ballast on main lines is usually lighter than that found in yards and service areas, which is sometimes almost black. You can blend colors and mix them to achieve variegated shades and great results.

Some commercial ballast is made of ground rubber, so it's light and easy to use. That's the type Dick and I chose for most areas of our layout. I know that some modelers like to use bird gravel or cat litter because it's cheaper, but who would want to put cat litter on a layout, particularly if there were cats in the neighborhood?

Applying ballast to your layout isn't difficult if you have the right tools—a pump-spray bottle (from Windex or some such product) and a household turkey baster. In addition, you'll need white glue, liquid dish detergent, and water. That's it.

With your fingers, work the ballast into a raised roadbed alongside and in between the ties. Smooth the ballast out at a level slightly below the tops of the ties. Try to get the loose pieces off the ties.

Fill your spray bottle with water and a few drops of detergent. The detergent breaks the surface tension of the water and allows it to penetrate more thoroughly than water alone will. Spray the ties and ballast generously with this "wet water" solution.

For a fixative, prepare a mixture of about 3 parts water to 1 part white glue. Add a few drops of detergent to this solution too. With the turkey baster, dispense a few drops of this mixture between each tie. It will run down and dry solidly in place in a day or two.

Be careful around switches and switch machines. You don't want to get the innards wet and the contacts coated with glue. Clean the rails with a ScotchBrite pad when everything has dried.

Our Atlas never shrugged

Dick and I decided to use contemporary, non-tubular track in the passenger terminal complex. Atlas came out with its new O gauge solid-rail system about the time we were building the benchwork for the terminal, which is visually isolated from the rest of the layout. Dick bought enough track, switches, and uncouplers to finish the project.

Before we were ready to install the Atlas system, we heard that some operators were having trouble with it. Apparently, the metal used for the rail joiners was too thin, which caused the joiners to loosen and provide only intermittent contact at best.

To circumvent the conductivity problems, I decided to bypass the joiners and feed each rail of every section independently from buses underneath the layout. Overkill? Perhaps, but I look at it as an ounce of prevention. The process is simple and repetitive. I cut out a section of the plastic web under each rail and soldered a 5" feeder lead to its bottom.

When Dick and I laid the track, we drilled holes for these new feeders. Then I strung bus wires for both the hot and ground cir-

Atlas O track looks terrific in the passenger terminal. To avoid potential conductivity problems down the road, John soldered feeder wires to each track section. The passenger trains glide in and out of the terminal flawlessly.

cuits under the benchwork and soldered the leads to them.

It worked. We've been using the terminal tracks for three years without a single flicker, hiccup, or stall. The trains run smoothly, even at realistically slow speeds, in and out of the station.

Keeping track of things

What kind of track should you use? Keep in mind that every type has benefits and disadvantages as you ask yourself:

• How much of a traditionalist am I? Should I stick with the old, reliable, traditional Lionel tinplate track?

• What about the venerable and more realistic GarGraves track with wooden ties and Ross switches?

• Would sectional track with roadbed already molded to it save a lot of work?

• Or how about Atlas' scale-looking three-rail track? It looks really good.

• Which switches and uncoupling sections from which manufacturer do I want to use?

• How realistic should the track look?

• Do I want to add ties? They enhance the appearance of tinplate track, which looks

Trackwork resources

Basic Trackwork for Model Railroaders by Jeff Wilson (12254)

Layout Plans for Toy Trains by Kent Johnson (10-8275)

Tips and Tricks for Toy Train Operators by Peter Riddle (10-8260)

Toy Train Layout from Start to Finish by Stanley Trzoniec (10-8305)

Track Plans for Toy Trains by Kent Johnson (10-8230)

Bridges over troubled water and other things

Just about every known bridge type appears on the LL/SF layout, spanning water, ravines, roads, and tracks. We have arch-under, bascule, girder, lift, trestle, and truss bridges, as well as a special kitbashed concoction Dick invented.

The bridges on the river are the most fun because they provide action and danger. Both are Lionel products made more than 40 years apart—a postwar bascule and an LTI vertical lift bridge, which we have tamed to work reasonably well most of the time. Visitors love them because they are noisy and brash.

We have a Lionel through-truss bridge on the layout, along with two old, repainted Marx trestles. Their upper members are slightly arched, as are some of the prototype Santa Fe bridges we've seen. Besides, they're made of metal and look old-fashioned. Even better, because they don't seem real substantial they have an air of "danger" to them.

Dick and I had to modify a few of the girder bridges to accommodate the track and the terrain. We sawed apart their bases with a hacksaw to make them wider for placement on a curve or wye. In a couple of cases, we used only half the bridge in the foreground—the other side was obscured or "implied."

Fact is, the other side was flush against the backdrop; that whole issue of track along a backdrop is a challenge!

Dick's own curved girder-on-trestle-piers invention spans the tracks leading to the transfer table and enginehouse. It's a 100-proof home-brew kitbash using curved strips of Homasote under the tracks, to the side of which HO girders are glued. All of this rests on Lionel trestle supports. Very clever and a good way to use up old trestle set pieces.

My favorite bridge is the one on the branch line to the oil facility. The line comes out of a tunnel in Mystery Mountain and crosses a dry wash on a Marx through-truss bridge. On the plate that identifies the bridge is the name "Trouble Water River." Another sign on the bridge prohibits fishing (for what, sand crabs?), swimming (on the dry bed sits an inner tube with a kid in it apparently waiting for a gully washer), and diving (stuck in the sand are two legs sticking straight up). In mid-air, suspended by "invisible thread" is a jumper headed, literally, for the river bottom.

The river got its name because "Trouble is, there's no water."—*John Grams*

Although LL/SF has no grades, the tracks cross other lines or rivers in many, many places. This one crossing over the engine terminal uses Lionel trestle set components (painted gray with rust streaks), Atlas HO scale bridge girders (painted gray) attached to two layers of Homasote cut to match the O-72 curve, and two Lionel plate girder bridges (one cut down the center and spread slightly because it's on the curve).

A repainted (but not weathered) Lionel Geep rumbles over Lake Dry Socket (in honor of John's dentist friend, Dave Watson) on the Trouble Water Bridge.

even better once you ballast it.

• Would track with roadbed attached be the best option for me?

So again, questions. Some have already been answered by earlier decisions. Others will be answered by decisions you'll make about rolling stock or scenery.

If things are starting to seem complicated, don't despair. Time is your ally. Remember that this is a hobby, and decisions are generally reversible. Take your time, daydream, relax, and think things through.

Control/Wiring: ZW or TMCC or DCS?

By John Grams

Acronyms and abbreviations—how could we ever live without them?
Even our toy train hobby has been turned into alphabet soup!

What the letters in the title eventually come down to is the horned dilemma operators face today: Do you want to use conventional control or command control (its modern counterpart)? Your choice can depend on a number of individual factors:

• Your overall layout concept. What do you want the thing to be? Are you more interested in the "hands on" aspects of operation, perhaps walking alongside the trains as they pound the main line? Or do you like to sit at the master control panel, fire 'em up, and watch 'em go? A little of both, perhaps? It's a personal matter.

• Your roster of rolling stock, particularly locomotives. What do you have now, and what are your plans for future additions? Can your favorites be converted to the new technology? Or will you need to relegate your postwar treasures to the display shelves?

• Your comfort level with the world of computer-type devices. Would you be at ease running your trains with a keypad instead of a throttle handle? Today's command control systems are amazingly versatile—capable of many more functions than the average operator will ever use—and come with 120 pages of instructions to prove it. The level of sophistication can be confusing and actually get in the way.

Of course, if you have your heart and mind set on going with the latest command-control technology, by all means do it. You'll be in for some great, realistic operation and sound effects, once you get the hang of it.

However, if when it's time to pick up a hammer and saw you still haven't decided between command control and conventional control, go with the simpler solution. Set up and wire your layout for conventional control first. That way, you can get all the low-tech bugs out before going on.

You can always add Lionel TrainMaster Command Control (TMCC) later if you are so inclined. The TMCC system has been around for almost a decade and is engineered to be compatible with existing conventionally wired layouts.

Four other manufacturers—Atlas, K-Line, 3rd Rail and Weaver—offer TMCC-equipped products. MTH does not.

The new MTH Digital Command System (DCS) has its own wiring requirements and may or may not be easily installed on existing layouts. It depends on the layout.

The DCS system is based upon circuitry carefully designed not to infringe upon any of Lionel's patents. Although DCS is supposed to do essentially the same things as TMCC, the electronics principles and devices are substantially different from one another. Compatibility issues, if they exist, are beyond the scope of this work.

On our LL/SF layout, Dick and I elected to go with conventional control initially and perhaps incorporate TMCC later on. That decision gave us a good chance to chase all the low-tech bugs out of the system before we exposed the layout to a swarm of the more sophisticated, computer-generated, electronic insects.

Our layout has run so reliably and smoothly on plain old transformer juice for the past several years that I doubt we'll ever convert to command control. After all, toy train railroads have been pleasing operators with conventional controls for a century. Why mess with a classic?

But that's the way we came down on the question. You'll need to do some reading (two good books are listed at the end of this chapter) and ask a lot of questions.

One O gauge switch uses 10 watts by itself.

Power in reserve

The main consideration to keep in mind when building a large layout—whether command or conventional-controlled—is to have plenty of transformer capacity. You'll want enough to handle several big locomotives and strings of illuminated cars, as well as all the lights and accessories dotting the landscape, without blinking or flinching.

It's no fun if your hotshot slows to a crawl when the whistle blows or it reaches the far side of the spread. It's even worse when overloaded internal circuit breakers kick in and out, giving the locomotive a sudden case of apoplexy, the only cure for which is shutting down the operation until the transformer coils cool.

The can-style motors in today's locomotives are more efficient than the old AC/DC universal motors found in most postwar models. Nevertheless, it takes fewer watts than many people realize to tax even the larger transformers to capacity.

According to the *Lionel Service Manual*, a basic O gauge single-motor postwar locomotive will draw 20 to 25 watts pulling an "average" train (whatever that means). The more cars in the consist, the more the wattage drain. A whistle adds 10 watts, a smoke generator 5 more. We're talking about 35 to 40 watts for just one typical train.

Automatic accessories consume 10 to 15 watts each, with some operating items taking up as much as 25 watts. One O gauge switch uses 10 watts by itself. Even the lowly 12- to 18-volt light bulbs draw 3 to 5 watts apiece. It adds up quickly.

So, a dual-motored diesel, with four illuminated passenger cars in tow, needs 80 to 90 watts just to leave the station. We haven't included automatic couplers and operating cars here because their current draw is momentary.

Before you start adding up these numbers and deducting them from your 275-watt ZW, remember that the wattage rating of a transformer is measured at the input. Under load, the amount of usable wattage available at the output is somewhat less. It is inversely proportional to the amount of amperage being drawn by everything—trains, lights, and accessories—connected to the transformer at a given point in time.

Here, from the pages of the *Lionel Service Manual*, are the usable wattage specifications for some popular postwar transformers. The amperage figures represent the maximum draw available before the circuit breakers kick in:

Type	Input Rating	Usable wattage at output
ZW	275 watts	180 at 14 amps
Z	250 watts	180 at 14 amps
KW	190 watts	140 at 10 amps
VW	150 watts	110 at 8 amps
V	150 watts	110 at 8 amps
LW	125 watts	75 at 5-6 amps
RW	110 watts	70 at 5-6 amps
1033	90 watts	60 at 5 amps

Dick and I agreed that the transformers assigned to running the trains would not be overburdened with add-ons. From the outset, we separated them from the ones that powered the lights and accessories. Then, as the layout, train, and accessory rosters expanded, so did the transformer complement.

> ### Key control and wiring questions
>
> - Am I going to use conventional/traditional control or opt for command control?
> - Do I want to walk around with the trains, or will my layout work better from a control panel?
> - If I choose command control, will I need to buy (or equip) new locomotives?
> - Am I reasonably electronically/electrically astute?
> - How much power am I going to need for lights, motors, etc.?
> - What gauge wire should I use?
> - Should the wire be solid or stranded?
> - Should I buy multiple colors of wire to make tracing easier?
> - How heavy should the electrical switches be?
> - If I've chosen to go with conventional transformers, do I understand phasing?
> - Should I use block wiring for the layout?

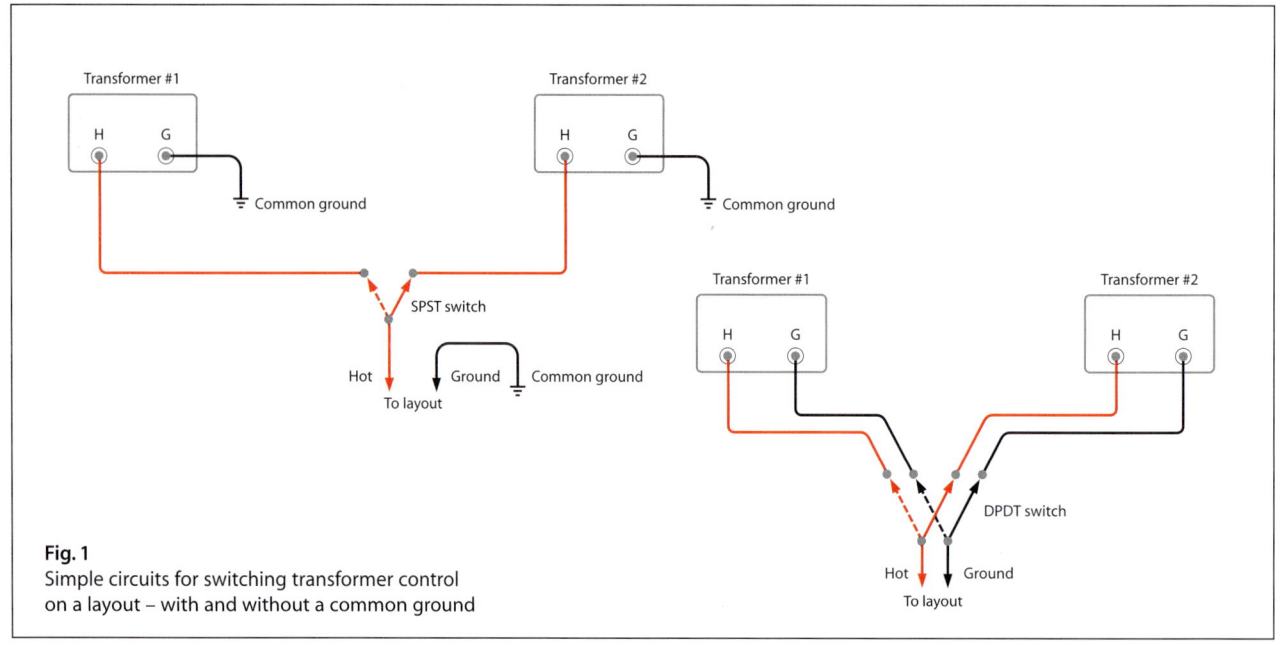

Fig. 1
Simple circuits for switching transformer control on a layout – with and without a common ground

Many operators underestimate the reserve power needed when their layouts are in full operation.

Today it takes nine transformers (plugged into three different household current circuits) to power the LL/SF layout.

• A Right-of-Way Industries 400-watt, dual-control behemoth handles both the upper and lower main lines.

• The lower main can be switched over to one side of a Lionel 275-watt ZW located closer to the locomotive-servicing facility and the passenger terminal.

• The other side of the ZW runs both legs of the wye, the coal and lumber spurs near the river, the enginehouse tracks, and transfer table.

• A Lionel 110-watt KW moves traffic in and out of the passenger terminal.

• A Lionel 175-watt LW takes care of shunting in the freight yards and the switchback lead to the oil plant.

• A Lionel 90-watt 1033 keeps the trolley running.

• At first, a 16-volt accessory circuit was powered by an American Flyer 100-watt transformer. When the breaker began to pop under the load, we replaced it with a Flyer 150-watt 9B. When that one became insufficient, we upgraded to a Flyer 250-watt 12B.

At that point, we decided to install another separate 16-volt circuit to serve future accessory needs and hooked the 9B to it. So, we have 400 watts of capacity just for the lights and accessories, not including the track switches and their controllers. The 34 switches are powered separately at 20 volts by a Lionel 250-watt Z.

• The choice of 16 volts for the accessory circuits was a kind of happy medium—I hate to say "compromise"—arrived at by taking into account the recommended voltages for the various accessories on the layout.

Only one accessory, the Lionel no. 362 barrel loader, gave us trouble. No matter how we adjusted the vibration motor, it still spilled more barrels than it delivered at 16 volts. We solved the problem by giving the thing its own power supply in the form of a 40-watt starter set transformer, which could independently be adjusted to a lower voltage.

That's a total capacity of 1,740 watts. Overkill? Dick and I don't think so. Everything works fine and runs cool, no matter how many trains and accessories we fire up. Many operators underestimate the reserve power needed when their layouts are in full operation. This is a common frustration we were aware of and swore we wouldn't have.

Our layout has control positions that are physically and visually separate. Therefore, we installed a selector switch that enables operators to shift control from one position to the other – the lower main line from one transformer position to the other. Here's

> **Control and wiring tips**
>
> - If you're unsure about command control, wire your layout for conventional control first. You can always add command control later if you wish.
> - Have enough transformer wattage capacity to handle all the trains, lights, and accessories you will use.
> - There are four basic theories of layout wiring—all of them work.
> - Don't overestimate the handling capacity of the wire you choose—bigger is better.
> - Color-code your circuits and be consistent.
> - A common ground bus can save you money and headaches.
> - Bus wires also work well on accessory circuits.
> - Heavy, industrial-grade toggle switches are a good investment.
> - If you use multiple transformers, they must be "in phase" with each other.
> - Automatic train control can be accomplished with relays and insulated blocks.
> - Wiring your layout in simple blocks has advantages even if you don't want automatic train control.
> - Several remote-control track sections can be wired together to conserve control panel space.
> - Lionel track switches need their own fixed-voltage circuits.
> - Insulated track sections operate lights and accessories better than contactors do.

how we did it:

Because we utilize a common ground, a single-pole single-throw (SPST) switch and only one wire were needed. Without the common ground, two wires and a double-pole double-throw (DPDT) switch will do the trick. (See fig. 1.)

Four theories of layout wiring

Before we get too deep in the matter of the controls, let me explain the four basic theories of layout wiring. The first two have to do with placement of the wires; the others are concerned with making connections. There are many variations on these themes, but we all seem to gravitate toward one or two of them to the exclusion of the others.

• Felix Unger/Mr. Clean approach. All the wiring is bundled together in neat cables that run only in straight lines along the whole length of the layout. Attachments are made at right angles. Nothing is hanging down, and not one strand is out of place. Clamps and cup hooks secure everything to the underside of the benchwork.

• Oscar Madison/Pythagoras approach. The rationale is that the shortest distance between two points is a straight line, so single wires run in all directions. This is the simplest way – it's direct, saves wire, and makes tracing circuits easy. Who's going to look under the benchwork anyway? This ain't the bridge club!

• Bill Gates/R2D2 approach. This is high-tech all the way and can become costly on a large layout. Wires have crimped lug fasteners at both ends and run individually or in cables to large terminal blocks, strategically spaced throughout the layout.

Proponents find this system esthetically pleasing and often belong to the same psychological Gestalt as those in the first category above. They argue that using terminal strips makes the layout easy to dismantle. I thought we were "mantling" here!

• John Wayne/Blazing Soldering Guns approach. Ah, the smell of gunsmoke and hot lead (not to mention rosin). Maybe it's a macho thing. Proponents of soldered connections swear by them and have a long history to back up their position. Soldered connections stay put and rarely deteriorate, even after decades of use.

Does soldering require a bit of acquired skill? Yes. Is it messy? Yes. In fact, if you've decided to go with carpeting on the floor, be aware that hot solder will burn holes in the threads. Protect them accordingly. On the other hand, soldering may just be the most practical choice.

As you might gather from our treatment of the four theories, the LL/SF leans toward the Oscar Madison and John Wayne approaches. We did install a couple of small terminal strips and cup hooks, so all the bases are covered.

Soldered connections stay put and rarely deteriorate, even after decades of use.

Choosing wire and switches

Give some thought to the broad principles of wiring, but you can worry about the details when you're ready to start crawling around under your benchwork. Here are some questions that will get you started thinking in general terms.

How heavy should the wire be? Please don't make the common mistake of overestimating the current-handling capacity of the wire you choose. Just as a larger-diameter pipe will allow for a greater flow of water, a heavier gauge of wire will do the same thing for the flow of electricity. There will be enough power loss in the tracks themselves – you don't need to lose even more in the wire leading up to them.

Remember: with wire, bigger is indeed better. Also, you can't have too many heavy-gauge track feeder wires on a large layout.

Consequently, Dick and I recommend using:
• 12- to 14-gauge wire for power buses
• 16-gauge minimum for track feeders
• 18- to 20-gauge for short runs to lights and accessories

Should the wire be stranded or solid? There's probably not much practical difference on a toy train layout, although some operators claim that stranded wire is a better conductor. It boils down to personal preference in each application. We used both.

Is it necessary to color-code my wire? Necessary? No. Advisable? Yes. Buy wire in as many different colors as you can, and assign a specific color to each application. Be consistent. This will make for easy tracing if problems arise.

Different sources have different colors and shade variations. For example, we used black wire for all ground connections, red for the "hot" center rail connections, white for the fixed 20-volt circuit feeding the track switches, and green on the first fixed 16-volt accessory circuit. When we had to add another accessory transformer, we installed dark blue wire for it. Other colors were used for track blocks, accessory leads, uncoupling tracks, and the like. One can run out of colors in a hurry.

Is there a general order to follow? The first thing Dick and I did was string 12-gauge electrical buses of solid wire in black, white, and green (for the common ground, switches, and accessories) around the circumference of the layout, 1 or 2 feet from the edge of the benchwork. This allowed for short feeder runs to almost any place.

Because of block wiring, we decided against a red third rail bus. Instead we ran red 16-gauge feeders from the transformers to the various positions in the track.

I recommend making notes that indicate the color codes and connections, then creating a master guide from your notes for later reference. A few years from now, it will be hard to remember what you did.

What do I need in the way of electrical switches? Particularly for those switches connected to track power, heavy-duty toggles work best. Itty-bitty hobby switches don't have the current-handling capacity needed here. Choose industrial-strength toggles with a rating of at least 10 amps at 120 volts. They'll probably still be working when you're long gone.

Using a common ground (return)

This is perhaps the most important consideration when designing the electrical circuits for your layout, particularly if it's a large one. A common ground means that the lights, the accessories, and one side of every circuit on the track (usually the running rails) are all tied together. So are all the transformers.

This arrangement simplifies making connections. It also saves on wire since only one long run, instead of two, is usually needed

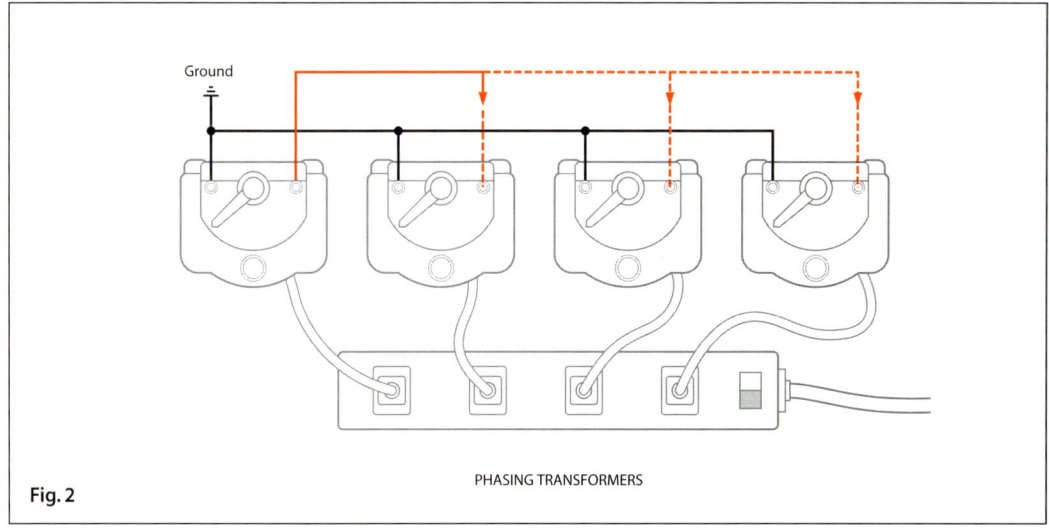

Fig. 2 PHASING TRANSFORMERS

for each item.

Our layout has five variable independent track circuits, two separate 16-volt light and accessory circuits, and one 20-volt circuit to power the switches linked by a common ground bus that encircles the layout 2 feet inside the edge of the benchwork. The ground posts of our transformers are connected to it at points on the layout.

Don't ask me how it works! Fortunately, electricity is smart and always finds the shortest path home on the bus wire, no matter how many different power sources are connected together in this way.

Finding the ground terminal post is easy on the larger Lionel transformers. Each is labeled "U" and often has internal common grounds built in. American Flyer called these same connectors "Base Posts."

Smaller transformers with only two terminals don't usually have a ground designation as such. In that case, pick one to be the ground. It doesn't matter as long as all the transformers are in phase with each other.

Phasing transformers

This basic concept is sometimes not fully understood by operators who attempt to use more than one transformer on their layouts. Simply put, like a team of horses, the transformers must be hitched up so that they can all pull in the same direction.

If the transformers aren't in phase with each other, trains will run erratically and short circuits may occur. This is the case even if a common ground isn't being used.

Test the phasing by connecting the grounds on two (or more) transformers. Plug them in and turn up their throttles. Attach one end of another wire to the hot terminal on one transformer, and touch the other end to the corresponding terminal on the second. If a spark is generated, the units are not in phase. Reverse the plug on one of them and try again. There should be no spark. Perform the same test as you add transformers.

Rather than switching wires around, transformer phasing is most easily done at the 120-volt wall outlet. If the two units aren't in phase with each other, reverse the line plug on one of them. After that, always insert the plugs into the outlet in the same way. (See fig. 2.)

Most operators find using switched multiple-outlet bars handy. That lets them leave transformer plugs inserted once the phasing is accomplished. They'll also be able to turn the power on and off at the terminal strip switch.

Block wiring

Whether or not you section off your main line for simultaneous multiple-train operation, you'll probably have to do some block wiring if you plan on having more than one thing happening at a time on your layout. Assuming you have a good idea of what your track plan will look like, or have already planned it, now's a good time to think about

Most operators find using switched multiple-outlet bars handy.

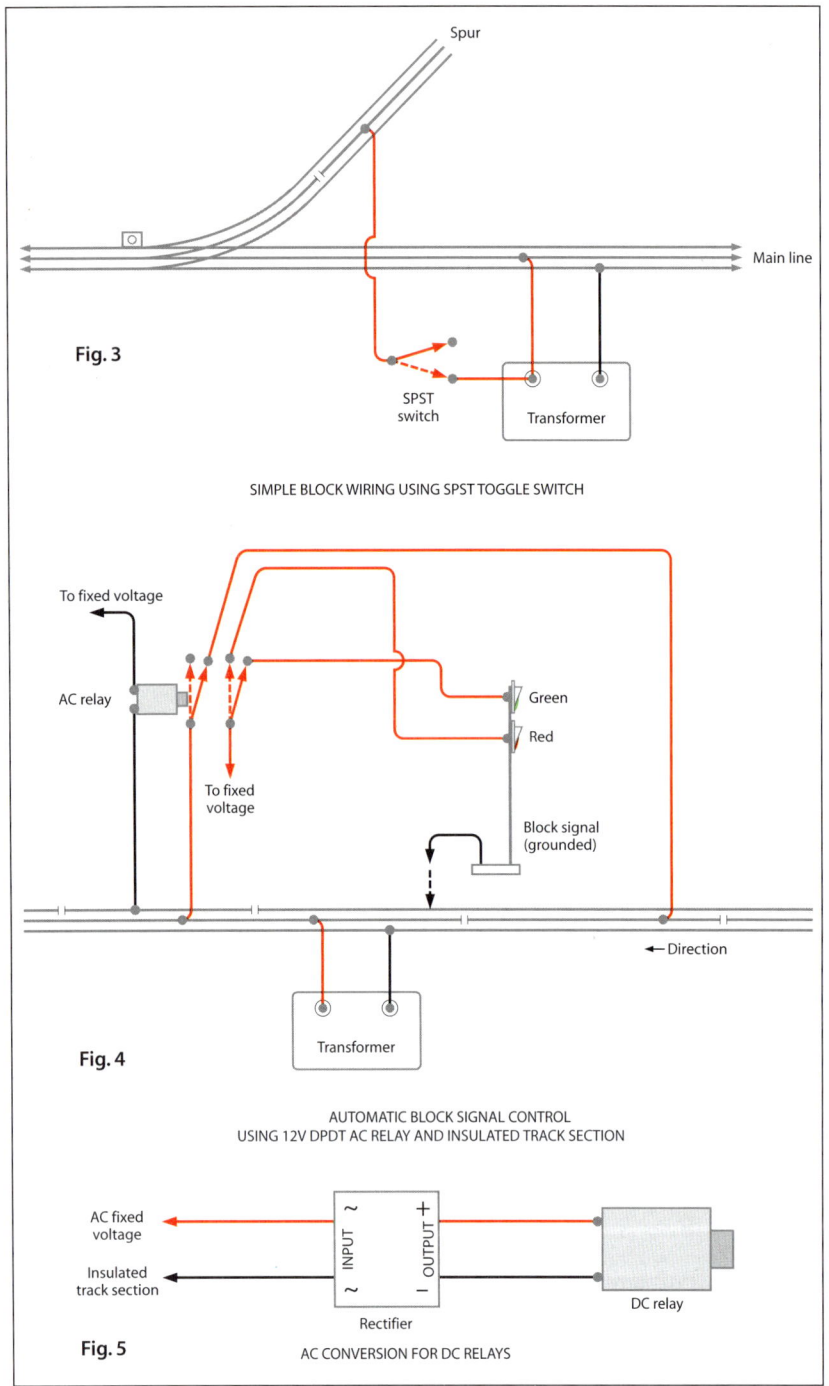

Fig. 3 — SIMPLE BLOCK WIRING USING SPST TOGGLE SWITCH

Fig. 4 — AUTOMATIC BLOCK SIGNAL CONTROL USING 12V DPDT AC RELAY AND INSULATED TRACK SECTION

Fig. 5 — AC CONVERSION FOR DC RELAYS

A separate feeder wire is then run from the insulated block, through an SPST toggle switch, to the transformer. Throwing the toggle to "off" halts everything in the block, from a locomotive to an entire train. The sidings and spurs on most layouts are hooked up this way, so trains can be held there until needed. (See fig. 3.)

Automatic mainline block control can be achieved by substituting an electrical relay for the manual toggle switch. The presence of a train in the block ahead trips the relay and cuts off power to a train that may be following until there's enough space between the two of them for both to run safely on the same track.

This kind of action has long been a favorite of some operators. For years, Lionel produced a pressure-sensitive contactor (generally unreliable and constantly needing adjustment) to achieve it. Operators today prefer the more-reliable performance of relays, activated by insulated track sections, to detect trains on their block-divided main lines.

The hookup shown in fig. 4 is for a 12-volt AC relay. Though still available, AC relays in this capacity are getting hard to find. You'll be able to find 12-volt DPDT DC relays at most consumer electronics stores. You can substitute a 12-volt DC relay, but you'll need at least a 4-amp, 50-watt, full-wave bridge rectifier ahead of it, wired as shown in fig. 5.

Watching two trains automatically run on the same track without crashing into each other can be fun, but it has a drawback. The reversing units of all the locomotives involved must be locked in the "forward only" position, thus eliminating any reverse operation until someone throws the lockout lever manually. That destroys the magic.

Dick and I debated the question of multiple-train main lines with or without automatic block signal control before deciding against it. Having planned on highballing fairly long trains, we thought that once a train entered the main, it should run continuously until we wanted it to stop, switch off into a siding, or break up in the yards.

We had two main lines, the upper and the

where you're going to want electrically isolated blocks.

Simple manually controlled blocks are usually created by insulating all the track sections in the block from the rest of the layout with insulating track pins. These can be made in two ways—by insulating the center rail or by insulating both running rails in the same way. While both systems have their own applications, benefits, and disadvantages, most operators end up choosing the center-rail method.

6

Scenery and Structures: Everyone can be an artist

By Dick Christianson

Over the first five chapters John and I have offered ideas to help you plan and design a better layout, select benchwork that works for you, lay track so the trains perform flawlessly, and wire a layout to achieve the most reliable performance from your trains. Now it's time to dress up the layout.

With the exception of the track plan, most aspects of layout building are pretty much invisible to everyone but you. It's only when you apply scenery and structures to a layout that you have something unique. For some hobbyists who get good at it, scenery becomes, well . . . art! It's the point where a layout begins to look like a miniature world. It's the payoff.

Choices about scenery

As stressed earlier, many of the choices available to you for scenery and structures were determined as you planned your layout. As you selected the space for your trains, you narrowed your choices for scenery and structures. For example, if you build your layout in a spare bedroom, you may decide that you aren't going to have room for the

Simple, neat, no-fuss scenery

The raw material for the underlying framework on our layout is corrugated-box cardboard, cut into 1" strips, which are then woven like a basket and tacked down to form the mountains and the valleys.

It's a good idea to run each strip over the edge of a table to break down the stiff fibers and make it more pliable. Your basket-weave pattern should be fairly tight, leaving no more than an inch or two of space between the strips. Dick used hot glue on all the joints and relied on spring-loaded clothespins to keep them together until the glue hardened. More than once he proved with burns on his fingers that hot glue is aptly named!

After removing the clothespins, Dick applied Woodland Scenics plaster gauze over the cardboard framework. He would cut off a piece about 12" long, dip it in a bucket of warm water briefly, and drape it over the cardboard structure. While the plaster was still wet, he spread it from the gauze and smoothed over the joints with his fingers. Then he let everything dry.

Next came the Hydrocal application. This product forms a hard shell when it dries. It's available in large bags from home and building supply stores. Dick and I used most of an 80-pound bag on the layout; so don't worry about the quantity you may have to buy. It's well worth the investment.

We mixed the Hydrocal with water until we had a soupy consistency—about as thick as a good grade of latex paint. Then we lightly sprayed the gauze with water. Next, we brushed the Hydrocal over the plaster gauze with a fairly heavy coat. We worked quickly because the Hydrocal sets up in the bucket.

You may want to apply a second coat of Hydrocal (again misting the surface first) for hardness and thickness. Once the scenery has dried, it can be painted in any color or combination, depending on the area of the world being modeled. Because we wanted a desert motif, we used a sandy beige flat wall latex.

Before the paint has dried, you should sprinkle on sand, dirt, grass, ground foam, and whatever else is needed to create the terrain you want. We used about 100 pounds of bulk sand, a little ground foam, and some lichen.

When the paint has dried, we recommend misting everything with a solution of about 15 parts water to 1 part white glue. Dampen it good. Plant sprayer bottles or an empty Windex bottle work well. The water/glue mix affixes everything to the surface, and we could even vacuum up the dust.

That's all there is to it! I guess this scenery process really is pretty simple. It's relatively neat, and it doesn't involve a lot of fuss. Dick was right after all!—*John Grams*

Shown here is the outside of Mystery Mountain, nothing more than a web of cardboard strips. Hot glue works well for affixing them, but remember—hot glue is hot. Cover the web with moistened plaster gauze strips (shown on the view inside Mystery Mountain). When the strips have dried, cover the gauze with a soupy plaster mix, add a coat of paint, sprinkle on ground cover, and you have a mountain.

Lionel lift bridge, which occupies a lot of territory and dominates a scene.

Your choice of a bedroom-sized layout also dictates that your track plan will be restricted to fairly small curve diameters. No Union Pacific Big Boys and Turbines. No long climb over Sherman Hill and wide-open Wyoming-style scenery. More likely, you'll be running small locomotives, maybe Geeps or switchers.

How about a layout featuring some city switching? Have lots of Union Pacific equipment? Maybe you can't model the entire engine-servicing area at Cheyenne, but you can still have some prairie running that allows you to create the barren hills and rocky bluffs characteristic of Wyoming.

When John and I began to work on our half-a-basement-sized layout, I had thought about what I wanted the layout to be and do. Half would be toylike, making use of the old Lionel accessories I had and a few more I'd acquire.

The other half of the layout (on the other

Building flats from paper and plastic

A great variety of HO scale backdrops is available—everything from cities, towns, and farms to mountains, prairies, and oceans white with foam. But if you're looking for something suitable for O gauge, good luck. There just isn't that much around.

So, Dick and I bought the scenes we wanted in HO scale and began experimenting with the enlargement feature on a four-color copier. We blew up scenes to a number of sizes to give us the illusion of distance and perspective. We trimmed away the sky and glued the panoramas to our blue backdrops.

Some of the illustrated buildings we wanted to appear closer. We enlarged the images still more (no formula here, just experimentation) and cut them out along the roof outlines. Next, we used 3M Spraymount to affix the cutouts to ¼" Fome-Cor to give an illusion of depth and edged them with black Magic Markers.

We glued a block of wood at the base of each cutout so it would stand unsupported. The block also served as a spacer to keep it away from the backdrop.

For a little different backdrop twist, we did something we hadn't seen done elsewhere. Dick has display shelves about 6" or 8" above the layout over the passenger yard. The wall directly behind the yard underneath the shelf looked bare. Then inspiration struck!

Dick remembered that, when rolling into the Amtrak terminal in Chicago from Milwaukee, there are the brick walls of what once was probably a freight terminal. We had a couple walls from an O gauge Lionel freight house (with side doors) that reminded us of Chicago.

Dick made full-size copies of the walls of a plastic freight station kit, complete with doors and windows, and we spliced them together. Next, we mounted them to a sheet of posterboard, cut them out, and tacked them to the wall.

Our project makes the passenger terminal look busy and realistic. In model railroading, necessity indeed breeds invention, and a little Yankee ingenuity helps.—*John Grams*

When you include a backdrop on your layout, you're invariably faced with the problem of adjacent tracks. Commercial backdrops work well—certainly better than anything our two authors could have painted. Painting the backdrop blue was enough of a challenge!

A variation of the paper backdrops worked well beneath the display shelves over the passenger terminal. Plastic walls from a freight station kit served as the basis for this long freight house next to the terminal.

Key scenery and structure questions

- What style of toy train layout do I really want: traditional, traditional with scale-like scenery, or scale everything except for three-rail track?
- Do my track plan and my vision call for mountains or prairie running?
- Do I envision my layout featuring deserts? Snow-covered mountains? Forests? Wheat fields? What's the general region the railroad runs through?
- What's the cost of the scenery I envision?
- Will building that kind of scenery be time-consuming?
- Do I have the skills needed to build it? Will I be able to learn the techniques?
- How neat does the scenery-building process have to be?
- Do I want to use operating accessories, or is that too toylike?
- Will the layout have a backdrop? If so, how will I finish it? Will trains have to go through it?
- Will my layout have city scenery (i.e., buildings) on it?

side of the backdrop) would be as close to a scale model railroad as John and I could go. That part of the plan changed a lot as we allowed toylike equipment and accessories to migrate, but at least we started out in a clear direction. On that side of the layout, we'd have big curves to play with. We also knew that it was going to be, at least in part, Santa Fe through the deserts of the Southwest. That meant lots of sand.

Because the layout was going to be two independent loops, one passing over the other, and all of this divided down the middle by a Masonite backdrop, there would be hills and rivers: i.e., scenery with contours. Another key factor was my preference for the Santa Fe. I already owned locomotives and rolling stock appropriate to that railroad.

Those were the broad strokes, the "givens." With those "predetermining" factors, in my mind's eye, I could look at my track plan and visualize the scenery (in general) as it would eventually appear on the finished layout.

Detailing the Inside of Tunnels

The insides of tunnels have long been overlooked, perhaps on the theory that whatever may be in there is in the dark and hidden behind the portal. You can go a long way with black paint, but if a viewer can see inside, the illusion disappears.

How you choose to detail the inside of your tunnel depends on the scene you are trying to create. Just be sure the interior decoration goes far enough that a viewer's perspective is covered from every angle. Use black paint deep inside if you wish, but the area immediately behind the portal should have some stonework, brickwork, or concrete liner.

We used commercial chunks of lightweight gray rock in several tunnels with convincing results. We weathered and blended it into a darker color toward the tunnel interior. In most cases, we needed to show rock only 4" or 5" into the tunnel. It's a neat effect and looks better than the underside of the cardboard strips and plaster gauze. —*John Grams*

From this angle, it looks like the rock face of Mystery Mountain was cut through to give the railroad access to the other side of the mountain. The second photo shows how short the rock vein was. Nothing more than a chunk of a commercial foam rock face.

Once you start making preliminary decisions, you'll be able to do it, too. In fact, I'll bet that by this point in the book you already have a pretty good idea of what your next layout's going to look like and how it will operate.

If you're still a bit awash with regard to scenery, let's see if we can take a logical look at the process. What kinds of questions do you need to ask – and answer – before you start mixing plaster? What do the choices you've made so far (track plan, space available, personal likes and dislikes, one-train operation or multiple) say about the scenery and structures you're likely to need?

• What kind of layout do you want to build? A realistically detailed layout that, but for the third rail, could be in *Model Railroader*? Do you want a flattop layout on indoor/outdoor carpet? Or do you want something between those two scenic extremes?

• Does your track plan call for a flat layout? Even if the track doesn't climb or descend, how about the scenery around it?

Scenery and structure tips

- Before you begin laying down plaster gauze, be sure you have a clear image of what you want the layout to look like.
- Consider doing a mock-up of the layout (clay model) to help you visualize where everything will go.
- Here's where having everything within reach helps. Make sure you have pop-ups or liftouts to give you access to every part of the layout.
- Don't be intimidated by scenery. You can do it. And if you don't like what you do in an area, rip it out and start over. Nothing's permanent.
- If scenery is new to you, read some books. Don't be afraid to read a model railroad-style book. Scenery on a two-rail layout doesn't need to be any different from scenery on a three-rail layout.
- Don't be afraid to get messy. Slop plaster around liberally. Paint with abandon (you can always paint over it).
- Talk to the owner and staff at your local hobby shop. They know what's new in scenery materials.

Roads to nowhere—or into the backdrop

Dick and I tried to create the illusion of distance in a number of ways, with varying success. Forced perspective isn't new to model railroading, but tricking the eye into perceiving depth in a scene is challenging, unless part of that scene is actually set back.

Two long expanses of building flats and masonry needed help. Both were either in the front of or behind the narrow shelf that carries the upper-level track along the backdrop. We broke the visual monotony by dividing the scene and installing girder bridges with roads under them.

Although the area under the bridge is only a few inches deep, the position of the vehicles suggests much more. Of course, to reinforce the illusion, the same type of scenic background should be visible as though continuing under the span.

I think the reason this visual scam worked so well was the placement of our trolley line. The streetcar actually disappears under upper main line bridges as it makes its way through the backdrop. Viewers see this happening, so it isn't much of a stretch of the imagination to believe the automobiles are doing the same thing.—*John Grams*

There's no hole through the backdrop here. The road makes a hard left behind the building flats and becomes unpaved plywood. You wouldn't know it from the photo though. Notice the buildings below and (apparently) behind the tracks and the half-girder bridge over the tracks. There's so much to look at that you don't question the reality of the scene.

Will there be rivers that need to go below layout level? What will the shape of the terrain be: depressions or gorges, flat, rolling hills, mountains?

• What will be on top of the scenery: Structures? Trees? Grass? Bushes? Sand? Remember that trees are expensive to buy ready-made; even if you choose to build your own, they still can be expensive and time-consuming. That's one of the reasons I've always preferred to model the Southwest—sand, low shrubbery, and a few cacti. Quick and relatively inexpensive to model, yet impressive as brightly colored trains contrast sharply against the monochromatic (i.e., mostly sandy brown) desert.

• How much time and money do you have? Can you afford to buy 300 built-up trees to save time? Or are your financial resources limited so that you'd be better off modeling the sandy desert or even just going with a carpet?

Solving the Mystery at Mystery Mountain

Dick and I painted $1/4$" Masonite blue to create a "sky" backdrop that divides the layout into scenes for easy viewing. Model railroaders in all scales have been using such simple installations for generations.

In some places, however, the track has to go through to the other side. Disguising these entrances and exits poses a problem. If not skillfully concealed, these fractures in the firmament could blow the effect of an entire scene. Ideally, the hole should be made out of a viewer's line of sight or hidden behind a building or hill. Tunnel portals can be used to great advantage.

Our easiest solution had the upper main line disappear behind a row of building facades on one side of the backdrop and emerge from behind a mountain on the other side. We also found that going beneath a bridge over an embankment or retaining wall drew attention away from and so minimized the effect.

The great building frame-up was a stroke of genius on Dick's part. Two tracks of the lower division disappear amid the crowded cluster of an industrial area. There are red brick structures on both sides of the right-of-way, with an extension of the complex overhead. The scene has to be three-dimensional, with the train being swallowed up between the factory buildings for maximum effect.

But without question, the masterpiece is the hidden automatic track-switching network on the upper level. We'd like to take credit for the illusion that goes on behind what we've come to call Mystery Mountain, but the neat effect was accidental as we sought to make the best of a difficult track/backdrop intersection.

Originally, the train was supposed to go 'round and 'round on the loop with a minimum of engineer participation. Then Dick got the idea to add two automatic non-derailing switches back to back, so the train would change routes and reverse direction with each pass.

Because the switches had to be positioned right in front of

Most visitors don't catch on to Mystery Mountain right away. Looking at it from here, you see that trains on the upper level go in the right and come out the left; another time they go into the left and don't come out; yet another time they come in from the left and don't come out; still another time they come in from the left and come out the right. It's all because of a pair of switches inside the tunnel (access from the other side of the backdrop). The authors didn't plan it to have this effect; they were just trying to hide the holes in the backdrop!

the backdrop, with two of the four tracks disappearing behind it, the only way we could hide this gigantic cavity in the wild blue would be by building a mountain over the whole thing, with portals on both ends. We lucked out.

As a train is seen entering one of the portals, logic and our senses indicate that it should exit the other one a few seconds later. It may or may not, depending on the way the switches are thrown inside the mountain (we have access to the switches behind the backdrop). It may appear on the other side of the backdrop or come around the loop from the opposite directions. Legerdemain from the book of Houdini! Having the mountain there adds a new dimension of mystery to the operation. Visitors love it, and it looks like we planned it that way.—*John Grams*

Likes are attractive.

It's perfectly okay to build a layout that mixes prewar accessories, postwar accessories, and modern craftsman kit structures. After all, it's your layout so do what you like.

However, since you bought this book to learn about building a better layout, let me suggest going with one style only. If you're into prewar trains, then such Lionel accessories as the nos. 164 log loader and 456 operating coal ramp are appropriate. Less so the no. 356 operating freight station. It's plastic and, though perhaps the right amount oversized, just doesn't fit with the metal accessories. And vice versa.

If you just can't part with some of your vintage accessories, an alternative is to group them. John and I did that to good advantage on our layout. For instance, I love the Lionel no. 364 conveyor lumber loader and 456 coal ramp. Together they look twice as good. Very near them we have a no. 395 floodlight tower. They look terrific as a group.

In front of the coal ramp, I placed a no. 397 coal loader. It's kind of a transition piece in that it's part metal and part plastic. Across the tracks is my childhood no. 145 automatic gateman—the blue giant! With its metal base and plastic hut, it works well.

The gateman is at the front of the layout, so the fact that he's enormous is perhaps less noticeable than if he were at the back of the layout. John and I even placed an oversized Volkswagen (maybe 1:32 proportion) waiting at the crossing gate next to the gateman. Looks about right.

So, at the front of the layout, we have a couple of large plastic-and-metal accessories and a little farther back there are comparably sized metal accessories. Beyond that we have the almost scale-size no. 192 railroad control tower with its small blue men, and beyond that we have a city scene of scale structures, figures, and vehicles.

From front to back there's a continuous "regression" from large to small, from toylike to scale. It works well, and John and I had fun making it work.—*Dick Christianson*

One secret to making tinplate accessories look somewhat natural with recent accessories and trains is to group things according to construction and size. In this case, the authors put the gate and gateman to the front (they're grossly oversized) and then installed the tinplate accessories (mostly metal but not terribly oversized) on the other side of the track. They put more scale-like accessories and structures farther back.

Paper backdrops, bridges, and tunnels

The divider plays a huge role in making our layout what it is. It begins on one wall of the basement, curves 90 degrees and runs in front of another wall, curves about 75 degrees and runs the entire length of the layout, curves back again about 75 degrees, and then 90 degrees. Looked at from above, the divider is a huge S.

Painted blue on the visible side (unpainted where it's not visible), the divider has a variety of paper backdrops attached to it. Those backdrops are different sizes and show different settings (cities, hills, buildings, river valleys, and more).

As neat and effective as a divider can be, it also creates scenery problems as the trains pass through it. These passages create gaping holes in the sky that challenged our ingenuity, but Dick and I managed to hide most of them pretty well.

The photos you see here are a little misleading because you can stare at them and say, "Well, they didn't do a very good job of disguising those holes." You may be right, but when you're visiting our layout and the trains are running, there's noise, and light, and motion to distract you. Seldom do your eyes rest on anything for more than a few seconds.

In more than one location, bridges go over the top of the hole so the train on the lower level seems to be going under a bridge, though in fact it's also going through the backdrop. Another hole is hidden by a hill that runs alongside the track perpendicular to the opening so that a train disappears behind a hill and then goes through the backdrop. You can't even see the hole in the backdrop.

A couple times we put a tunnel portal up against the backdrop. In those cases, the hole in the backdrop was beneath a girder or some other kind of bridge, so the very short tunnel doesn't seem too implausible.

Dick and I liked the illusions we were creating so much that we decided to see how blatant we could be about it. We even had a couple of roads go into the backdrop. One street goes under the track running along the backdrop and makes a hard left before it heads into buildings pasted to the backdrop. It's dark beneath the bridge, and the effect is good.

My favorite, though, is a gray road that crosses the tracks. It continues under a bridge and within 4" runs into the backdrop. Glued to the Masonite backdrop is a paper backdrop on which there's a gray street that continues into the scene. Almost seamless.

Model Railroader magazine's slogan since the 1950s has been "Model Railroading is Fun." Finding solutions to the holes-in-the-sky problem was a challenge, but it was fun. We kept running trains, talking about the problem, moving things around, and finally the solutions came. —*John Grams*

This neat scene is similar to one on the other side of the layout. It works because the road seems to continue on from the grade crossing, under the bridge, and into the backdrop.

Showing in this scene are four holes through the backdrop. At the left, the trolley cuts through beneath an arch bridge and through a tunnel portal; just beyond the signal bridge, the trolley line cuts through again beneath a girder bridge and with a curved brick wall on both sides. To the right, the main line and yard lead cut through beneath another girder bridge; on the upper level, a train heads into a tunnel that pierces the backdrop.

• How neat do you have to be? Can you sling plaster around without fear of retribution? Will you get in trouble if paint drips on the floor? How about tiny pieces of ground foam or little schnibbles of pink insulating foam?

The same predetermining factors that influenced your decisions regarding scenery will also affect the kinds of accessories and structures you add.

• Do you want to go mainly with Lionel, MTH, and K-Line operating accessories? Is the layout supposed to be about fun? Or is it supposed to be serious?

• Do you want it to look and feel like a scale model railroad? If so, will you be using Atlas, MTH, and Walthers ready-built structures? Or are you interested in building the more challenging "craftsman" kits?

• Do you want to see trains at all times? If not, then you may want a backdrop.

• Do you have the skills to paint your own backdrop? Should you buy paper backdrops

Scenery and structures resources

Basic Scenery for Model Railroaders by Lou Sassi (12233)

Building City Scenery for Your Model Railroad by John Pryke (12204)

How to Build Realistic Model Railroad Scenery (2nd edition) by Dave Frary (12100)

New Scenery Tips and Techniques by Kent Johnson (12243)

Realistic Plastic Structures for Toy Train Layouts by Art Curren (10-8050)

Scenery for Your Model Railroad by Mike Danneman (12194)

Tips and Tricks for Toy Train Operators by Peter Riddle (10-8260)

Toy Train Layout from Start to Finish by Stanley Trzoniec (10-8305)

Trackwork and Lineside Detail for Your Model Railroad by Kent Johnson (12235)

City built on styrofoam

The LL/SF needed an urban business block to serve as the focal point for the trolley line on one side. There was only one problem. The city had to be located in front of the backdrop, far from the edge of the benchwork.

To be convincing, the business district needed to be well detailed with three-dimensional buildings, a street, cars, signs, poles, fire hydrants, figures, and the like. It also had to fit within the trolley loop.

Dick decided that the only way this could be easily accomplished was if we built the thing in all of its detail on the workbench and set the entire block in place when it was finished.

We started with a piece of ¼" Fome-Cor that we trimmed to fit within the trolley loop. The buildings were stock Design Preservation Models O scale kits, with their interiors and floors painted black. In addition, we installed black tagboard baffles inside so it was hard to see anything through the large store windows. A number of exterior signs and window posters drew attention from the darkened interiors.

We painted the street and sidewalk in an aged-concrete gray color, which was continued on the road leading away from the block. For a touch of realism, joints and cracks were added to the "concrete" with a black Magic Marker.

We glued into place all the details, figures, poles, etc. at the

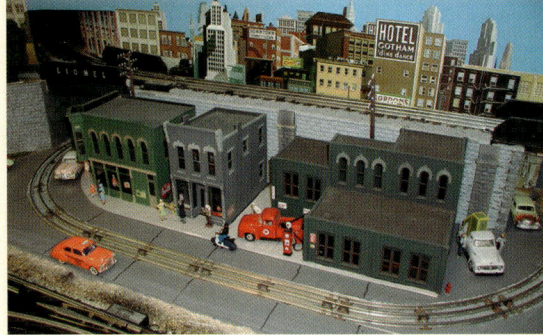

Not having the patience or stamina to spend a week of evenings up on the layout (those three rails dig into your knees!), John and Dick decided to build this city on a piece of styrofoam on the workbench. Once the structures, figures, and other details had been glued in place, it took only one trip on top of the layout to put it in place.

workbench. Vehicles were added after the scene was in place.

With the trolley loop acting as a natural dividing line, the commercial area looks as though it had always been there. Dick and I avoided needless hours of fussing, bending, and stretching by building it on the workbench.—*John Grams*

Making a fast and dirty river

The river was the last scenic feature Dick and I installed, mainly because we weren't sure which technique to use.

After extensive research, we discovered that there must be a dozen ways to create water on a layout. A metal trough with the real thing circulating, layers of clear epoxy over a painted river bottom, blue-painted plywood—modelers have tried just about everything.

When Dick and I finally got around to acting, we found ourselves under the gun. Visitors from the Lionel Operating Train Society would be coming in less than three weeks, and we needed something quick!

Procrastination bred a fortuitous decision. Bandleader Glenn Miller always said, "It's the simple things that swing," so that's the philosophy we adopted. After almost 10 years of fretting and indecision, the river was finished in four nights.

First, we applied a shallow, even layer of drywall cement, about 1/8" thick, over the sunken plywood "river bottom" and allowed it to dry for a day. Then we went back and smoothed it with a damp sponge.

Then Dick and I painted the drywall cement with Ace Hardware "Midnight Blue." Once that had dried, we followed with two coats of artist's gloss medium, which we swirled with a 6" x 8" damp sponge to give the water an agitated appearance in places.

As the finishing touch, we cut Brawa corrugated seawall along the banks. This product comes in rusty-metal-colored plastic, so only a minimum amount of aging and weathering was required.

After adding the water skier, shark, and partially submerged caboose under the Lionel no. 313 bascule bridge, we had created a credible if quirky river with a minimum amount of time and effort.—*John Grams*

The last piece of scenery to be completed was the river cutting through the engine terminal side of the layout. The river looks neither fast nor dirty, but the techniques to complete it are certainly fast—and easy. Plywood, drywall cement, paint, and gloss medium: four steps was all it took.

to apply to Masonite or even to a wall?

Over the years, John and I have seen innumerable layouts with track on benchwork and trains running, but devoid of scenery. When asked about it, the layout owner usually says, "I'm not an artist," or "I'm afraid I'll mess it up."

Please don't let your fears keep you from putting scenery on your layout. It's the most important thing you can do to bring your layout to life. Without scenery and structures you have a layout, but you don't have a model railroad. Give it a try.

Telephone poles—What they really look like

Telephone and, before that, telegraph poles, have been a conspicuous part of the right-of-way for almost as long as railroads have been around. Miniature poles, correctly constructed and carefully placed, can add an air of realism to any model railroad.

On Dick's last trip to the West, he took pictures of the prototype poles on the Santa Fe. He used those photos to guide him when modifying commercial O scale poles to create convincing lineside details.

What did he notice?

- Real telephone poles are shorter than the plastic models on the market. Many aren't much higher than the top of a train (often because they're placed at the base of a fill).
- Most of the poles he photographed had only one cross-arm.
- Poles tend to settle into the ground over time, resulting in some oddly tilted specimens.
- Poles aren't always at track level, particularly those near cuts and fills.
- Real poles don't have round bases with screw holes in them.

Armed with this information, Dick set out to customize the poles he had bought. First, he cut off their tops with a hobby saw, leaving only one cross-arm, and sawed off their round bases. He painted them a dull, weathered brownish-gray, then daubed the insulators with aqua paint (Penn Central green) to simulate their glass prototypes.

Placement on the model right-of-way was done according to eye appeal—whatever looked good. Dick and I ended up with poles that are spaced closer together than in the real world. They just look better that way. (Most things are selectively compressed in this hobby.)

Telephone poles are available from a variety of sources. Dick and John put a couple of them, unmodified, on the city on Styrofoam. But they aren't aware of any poles that look like those found along railroad main lines in the 1950s. A hobby saw works well for cutting arms off the poles and removing the bases. Tilting some poles and varying their height gives them a real-world look.

Dick drilled holes in the hardshell landscape and glued the poles in place. Before the glue had set, he tilted and twisted a few of them for the sake of realism.

Incidentally, the black streaks of what apparently is coal streaming down the side of the right-of-way at intervals, is based on a photo that appeared in *Trains* magazine a couple years ago. We don't know what it is or why it is, but if it was in *Trains*, it must be right!—*John Grams*

---

his echo. Do you suppose they're hearing the echo of their "hello" or just the other fellow's "hello"?

Maybe the yodelers aren't that goofy. Maybe it's an inside joke that only John and I will notice or care about, but that's okay, too. As a wise friend once told me, "Sometimes you just have to satisfy the inner man." And we're pretty satisfied with ourselves. Some evenings we spent most of three hours just wandering around looking for gags involving figures.

The real beauty of how this has turned out is that when you look at the layout as an overall piece of work, you don't notice the gags. It just looks like a big layout. But when you walk around the layout and slowly pick out the details, that's when the fun begins.

• Trees. Another area where you have many, many choices. I recommend getting a Walthers catalog or a catalog from Scenic Express catalog and spending some time flipping through it. You'll find evergreens in many sizes, along with deciduous trees of every shape and size. They come in kits and ready built. And, of course, as I said before, I recommend cacti, especially if time is of the essence to you. You don't need as many of these as you'll need trees if you model the Pacific Northwest, for instance.

• Miscellaneous stuff. Don't forget boxes, crates, baggage carts, suitcases, ladders, garbage trash cans, street signs, fire hydrants, street signs, street lights, police call boxes, and on and on. All of these things are "in nature," and manufacturers make them.

• Track and roadbed. Adding ties between the metal ones on three-rail toy train track goes a long way toward making the track realistic (if you ignore the third rail, of course). Years ago my dad and I had cut probably 500 ties on a table saw. A couple years ago John soaked all of them in a witch's brew of brown, maple, mahogany, black, and who-knows-what stain.

The ties took days and days to dry in the garage, but they finally ended up looking like creosote-treated railroad ties. We put some Elmer's glue on the underside of the ties and slipped them in (three or four) between the metal ties, applied ballast, and voila! A reasonably detailed right-of-way.

• Lineside details. The late Gordon Odegard, a close friend of mine and associate editor at *Model Railroader*, used to complain that modern railroads were no longer interesting to model. The water towers were gone, crossing towers no longer stood on guard—many of the distinctive features of railroads have gone away.

If you're modeling the 1940s, '50s, or early '60s, you still have plenty to work with. Later than that, though, the right-of-way gets pretty lonesome looking.

One feature found on most rights-of-way, though, is the telephone pole. I modified some plastic telephone poles, roughed them up with sandpaper, painted them a weathered gray, touched the insulators with Penn Central green (aqua), and spaced them out along the main line. They look pretty darned good for plastic line poles.

Another lineside feature you can still see is signals. Here's where I compromised my "scale" tendencies somewhat. I like Lionel's block signals and semaphores, so I used them. They look silly, but I don't care. I love the red and green lights, not to mention the semaphore arm. I can't help it, and I'm not ashamed of it. Of course, if I were to build a "better" next layout, I might consider purchasing and installing some of the gorgeous scale lineside signals and crossing flashers and gates that are on the market nowadays.

How far you want to go in the way of details is entirely up to you.

Detailing tips

- Details in the foreground should be plentiful and realistic; details further back need not be quite as ... well, detailed.
- If your trains range from highly realistic scale models to generally representational tinplate, then your figures, vehicles, and structures should be mixed as well.
- If you're trying to stick with scale-like trains, then your figures, vehicles, and structures should be scale-like too.
- Consider creating mini-scenes that viewers might not notice at first, but will be pleased to eventually notice.
- Consider making those mini-scenes humorous.
- Look around you. If you're modeling a city scene, drive around and observe city streets, buildings, sidewalks, and vehicles. Because you're looking for them, you'll see details you hadn't noticed before.
- Don't forget signs and billboards along the roads and on buildings. Use them to date and "locate" the railroad (e.g., a Lionelville City Limits sign).

Look around you

The choice is yours. How far you want to go in the way of details is entirely up to you. And the really beautiful thing about it is that you can just keep adding as long as you want.

"But," you may protest, "I don't have the imagination to do that sort of thing. How do I know what to put where?"

First of all, you really don't need much imagination. Others have been doing the imagining for you. Take the figure manufacturers, for instance. Arttista makes a figure of a mailman with a dog pulling on his uniformed pant leg. A great little story that would fit on any city street on your layout. Visitors absolutely love this sort of thing. Take a look at the figures and details at your hobby shop. You'll get tons of ideas.

Another approach is to go to a nearby railroad yard where you can find some public access. (Don't trespass. The railroads take security very seriously these days, and rightly so.) Take some pictures, if possible. Look at what's around and shoot some pictures.

Fun with figure placement

Finding the right figures to dress up scenes on your layout adds elements of life, movement, credibility, and realism to an otherwise static environment. They can even be funny, if you're so inclined. They reinforce basic railroad themes at stations, yards, and service facilities, not to mention other areas of the layout that might need a boost. In addition to the obvious railroad types that populate station platforms and environs, we added people doing their own thing elsewhere:
• Three guys in sweatsuits, obliviously jogging along the road. We dubbed them the Olympic Synchronized Jogging Team in Training—since they're in perfect synchronization being the same figure.
• An oil company executive sitting on top of the oil derrick, reading about Enron in his newspaper.
• A kid in an inner tube, sitting on the stones at the bottom of Lake Dry Socket, not caring that there isn't any water around. The possibilities for adding interest and fun with figures on your model railroad layout are limited only by your imagination. It's your own little kingdom – go wild! – *John Grams*

Here's another scene that doesn't sink in right away. Workers puzzle over what to do next as the two ends of the pipeline aren't going to line up. Flex-pipe perhaps? The two pipes are misaligned in every way. If you could read the sign, you'd find that Big Foot Pipeline Co.'s motto is "Excellence in Engineering."

This toy Winnebago cost too much—Dick bought it at an antique store—but it was the perfect detail to go in that spot on the layout.

John cut off part of a caboose shell gone bad, set it on the river under the bridge, and put an O scale engineer on the roof.

Now here's an old joke: water skiing behind a rowboat. The skis worn by the matronly bikini-clad lady are cardboard strips from Walthers Goo packaging.

Viewers assume the tow truck is trying to pull a submerged car out of the water, but the authors prefer to think that it's fishing for rather large fish.

Notice the light-colored sand along the tracks where locomotives have needed to gain some traction. How well-maintained is the right-of-way? Is there litter blowing around? What's that pipe sticking up out of the ground for? Wonder what those two guys near the yard office are doing: having a smoke? Just replicate what you see.

If you have access to books about railroading, flip through them. You'd be amazed at what you can see in photographs. Subscribe to *Trains* and *Classic Trains* magazines. They have lots of photos in them that are loaded with details!

Honestly, I could go on forever, but surely by now you've gotten the point—or points.

• First, the level of detail you choose for your layout is up to you.

• Second, the opportunities for details are everywhere in products that will beautifully enhance your layout.

• Third, have fun with the details—they'll give you and your visitors pleasure for years to come. And if you're the only one who seems to notice the motorcycle cop behind the billboard, it's okay. At least you've satisfied the inner man.

• Finally, when it comes to ideas for details on the layout, look around you. You're simply trying to suggest, replicate, and/or repeat what you see in the real world. You and visitors to your layout will enjoy recognizing "reality."

Detailing resources

Ideas from scale model railroading books
Model Railroad Bridges and Trestles (12101)
The Model Railroader's Guide to Locomotive Servicing Terminals by Marty McGuirk (12228)
The New Scenery Tips and Techniques by Kent Johnson (12243)
Realistic Animation, Lighting, and Sound by Kent Johnson (12199)
Trackwork and Lineside Detail for Your Model Railroad by Kent Johnson (12235)

Ideas from toy train books
Tips and Tricks for Toy Train Operators by Peter Riddle (10-8260)
Toy Train Layout from Start to Finish by Stanley Trzoniec (10-8305)

Rolling Stock: It looks better when it's all the same height

By John Grams

What kinds of rolling stock—motive power, freight, and passenger cars—should be on your layout? The answer to that is personal, depending on what you like, what you own, and perhaps what you want to keep of the things you own. This is why swap meets are so popular.

There are many other considerations that dictate rolling stock rosters.

• The size of your layout. A Union Pacific Big Boy and 80-foot scale Pullmans require more room than a 4 x 8-foot sheet of plywood. If your space is limited, look to smaller locomotives and shorter cars—it will make what you have seem larger.

• The type of operation. Will your layout be focused on a passenger station, a freight yard, an industrial complex, the open road, or maybe a combination of these?

• The locale. Do you want a big city, a small town, or a rural area? What section of the country—east, west, south, middle? Answers to these questions have a bearing on the composition of the traffic and indicate what rolling stock looks right in the scene.

• The era. Model railroads of all kinds in historical time frames are becoming popular. Maybe it's a nostalgic yearning for a better time. The 1940s through the mid-1960s are hot right now. Perhaps it's because this time represents a transition from steam to diesel power, so both can be run with abandon. This also was a time when railroads were the key to everyday life. There are thousands of reasons for period layouts.

• Favorite prototype railroad. Mythical branch lines of a real railroad are popular. Imaginary mergers are good too. Both give the opportunity to feature several road names.

Our "hostile takeover" of the Santa Fe by the Lionel Lines gives the widest latitude of all, because one of the merging partners is mythical, but it has a lot of rolling stock around bearing its name and herald. Besides, it gives us a chuckle now and then.

• Favorite consists. There are passenger trains, limiteds and locals; freight trains, transcontinental and peddler. Maybe you really like work trains. Don't ignore unit trains of all kinds. They have been with us for a long time, probably starting with coal and ore trains. We like them on the LL/SF and have two that run regularly—a livestock train, with a string of short cattle cars and an oil train consisting of double-dome tankers.

> ### Key rolling stock questions
>
> • Do you wish to be selective in your rolling stock or just run what you like?
> • If you want to be selective, on what will you base your selection? Uniform scale/size? Correct prototype era? Appropriate to the real railroad? Recent-production equipment?
> • Are you aware of compatibility issues among manufacturers?
> • Have you considered how your long, modern cars or 80-foot passenger cars will look on your O-31 curves? Have you allowed for plenty of clearance at tunnels, on curves, and between tracks on curves?
> • Are you aware of the operating qualities of specific locomotives?
> • Can you tolerate the appearance of modern equipment mixed in with vintage trains, particularly motive power?

• None of the above. There are some operators who don't care about the rules. They run anything and everything all the time and have a ball doing it.

The decision is entirely yours. Are you a purist who wants to operate a three-rail prototypically correct layout? Does anything go on your train table, or are you fastidious about some things but not others? As long as you make the rules, you can play the game any way you want.

O gauge rolling stock size differences

Anyone who's been around the oval a few times knows that Lionel made O gauge trains in a great variety of sizes and shapes. The only thing these products seemingly had in common was the distance between the track's running rails.

With its dominant position in the electric train field, Lionel had to produce trains on several levels to satisfy the sub-markets within the field. At one end were the "entry level" customers, up through several ranks of more sophisticated "repeat buyers," who needed something new to add or a "better" second set, all the way up to the "hobbyists," who took their toy trains seriously and built slice-of-life model railroads with them.

Lionel loved them all and tried hard to satisfy each and every one. It did this by making several classes of trains, corresponding roughly to size and price range. All of them ran on the same track and could be coupled together, but often the difference in apparent bulk made side-by-side comparisons seem ludicrous.

Over the years, Lionel manufactured essentially three classes (or sizes) of rolling stock: O-27 starter-set line (Type I), a middle-of-the-road-compromise line (Type II), and just before World War II and again more recently, a quarter-inch scale line (Type III).

Fortunately, most of the other manufacturers of today's trains have followed Lionel's lead. You can find some of their rolling stock corresponding to all three sizes. But let's use the more universally familiar Lionel products for our examples.

Here are some representative pieces from each class:

Type I

Locomotives: no. 1654/Scout-type 2-4-2 and nos. 1666/2026-type 2-6-2 steamers, Alco diesels.

Passenger cars: Sheet-metal heavyweights, short plastic streamliners.

Freight cars: 9 ¼" boxcars and stockcars, short gondolas, short metal flatcars, double-dome tank cars, SP-type cabooses.

Type II

Locomotives: no. 675-type 2-6-2 based on old no. 225E castings; Berkshire 2-8-4s and Hudson 4-6-4s based on old no. 226E castings; Santa Fe-type Hudsons; EMD F3s, Geeps, and NW2 diesel switchers; GG1 electrics.

Passenger cars: Heavyweight Pullmans, extruded aluminum streamliners.

Freight cars: no. 6464-type and similarly sized boxcars, long gondolas, sheet-metal single-dome and plastic triple-dome tankers, four-bay hoppers, bay window and porthole cabooses.

Rolling stock tips

- Tailor the type of rolling stock you run to your specific layout and kind of operation.
- Separate different sizes of rolling stock.
- Realize that operational incompatibilities exist between products of different manufacturers.
- Products of the same manufacturer aren't necessarily compatible with those made at different times.
- Most rolling stock incompatibilities can be overcome with a little experimentation and modification of the offending pieces.

Type III

Locomotives: no. 700E and similarly sized Hudson 4-6-4s, most notably no. 773; Pennsy-type 0-6-0 yard switchers; *Hiawatha* Atlantic 4-4-2s, Union Pacific streamlined diesels.

Passenger cars: None except the vestibuled streamliners.

Freight cars: Four famous prewar cars – boxcar, hopper, tank car, and caboose, some of which spilled over into the early postwar line; Standard O line made intermittently since the 1970s.

Many more full-scale Type III models have been produced within the last decade or so by Lionel, MTH, K-Line, Weaver, and others.

Type crossovers

Some pieces Lionel made were probably intended to be used in more than one series—usually Types I and II. Examples are the Turbine 6-8-6s and 0-4-0 steam switchers, Bucyrus-Erie cranes, coal dump cars, long flatcars, two-bin hoppers, work cabooses.

The rule of Noah

Most of us who have been in this hobby

There's only one O gauge, and there's only one O scale. All the Lionel K-Line, MTH, Williams, and Weaver cars and locomotives run on O gauge track because their wheels are all the same distance apart. But not everything all the manufacturers make or have made is O scale. In fact, as this photo shows, there's a big difference in the sizes of O gauge trains available. One way to improve your layout's appearance is to settle on one size of O gauge cars and locomotives. At least, avoid running them together end to end. For the most part, Dick and John run scale-size trains on the upper level and smaller-scale trains on the lower, but they're not too strict about this.

Compatibility factors

Dealing with real or perceived incompatibilities with the electronic control and/or sound systems of contemporary train manufacturers is beyond the scope of this book—way beyond! Perhaps some day they will share their patent rights in the spirit of preserving the hobby. The HO guys did that a long time ago, and look at how that field has grown. They realized there was room for everybody in the gondola if they all paddled in the same direction.

What happened with the Lionel magnetically actuated knuckle coupler a couple of decades ago proves the point. There is no question anywhere that Lionel invented the thing; it held the patents since the 1940s and updated them periodically.

With the start of the "tinplate renaissance" in the late 1970s, other manufacturers used crude dummy knuckles of the same size and shape to mate with Lionel couplers. In the 1980s, the other manufacturers began coming out with operating knuckles that looked like and worked like Lionel's. Today, every piece of new tinplate rolling stock has these couplers, and many have the fast-angle wheels too.

Did Lionel not notice or care what was happening? Not likely. Why didn't it take action? Perhaps its leaders were wise enough to realize that if the rolling stock of other manufacturers was compatible with theirs in this way, the hobby would grow. It did. Things have changed since then, unfortunately not necessarily for the better.

Switch incompatibility

A prevailing notion about toy trains holds that a seamless stream of progress and continuity stretch from the time J.L. Cowen installed the first electric motor in a train in his New York loft to today. This implies that everything in O gauge, for instance, should work with everything else. In spite of a conscious effort to achieve basic compatibility among the products of various manufacturers, glitches and hiccups do occur.

According to Ray L. Plummer, who

Most of us who have been in this hobby for any time have amassed an eclectic assortment of rolling stock of all three types.

for any time have amassed an eclectic assortment of rolling stock of all three types. Shelf displays pose no problem, but what do you do with them on a layout?

Follow the rule that Noah used to keep order on the ark: "To avoid chaos, each must be kept with its own kind." In other words, it's fine to have Types I, II, and III trains on the same layout, but don't mix the rolling stock on any one train.

The eye and the imagination can compensate while watching a train of Type I cars meet a train consisting of Type II rolling stock at a passing siding. As long as the trains are internally consistent, a slight difference in overall size between the two can be visually ignored. But watching a Type I locomotive pulling some Type III passenger cars around a layout is like watching clowns pile out of a Mini Cooper at the circus.

Whether to weather

Ten years ago, toy train modeler extraordinaire Joe Lesser and I embarked on a book project. The toy train hobby was flourishing, especially the collecting side, but Joe is a thinker who doesn't follow trends. Instead of collecting, he was an advocate of operating toy trains. He (with his wife JoAnn's enthusiastic support) built a large layout in their living room (California—no basement).

Classic Toy Trains magazine has published several of Joe's articles over the years. Inspired by his work, Kalmbach Publishing Co. published his book *Realistic Railroading with Toy Trains*, now out of print.

In an early chapter of that book, Joe offered a "levels of realism" continuum. It begins with three-rail tinplate track on a carpet and goes through tinplate track on painted plywood and then tinplate track with scale-like scenery and structures. Joe moves on to more-realistic track (GarGraves, Atlas, etc.) with scale-like scenery.

At the end of the continuum, Joe mentions realistically weathered structures and—gasp!—weathered cars and locomotives. I don't think anyone can argue that weathering trains makes them more realistic. The argument is not about the esthetics, but about the financial "wisdom" of doing it. Will it "ruin" the collector value?

As with everything else about this hobby, the decisions are personal. Here are some questions to ask yourself before you start weathering:
- How much money do I have for trains?
- Is eventual resale of my "investment" an issue?
- Will the layout I'm planning look better with weathered trains and structures?
- Am I a collector? An operator? Both? If I'm both, should I weather only the "runner-quality" trains?
- Should I weather only new equipment and not "ruin the collector value" of the old trains?
- Am I skilled enough at weathering that the appearance of my trains will be improved?
- Do I have a nostalgic attachment to the trains?

Not us

Perhaps you've noticed that John and I haven't weathered our trains and structures. Let me answer the questions above from my point of view.
- I don't have enough money for trains. Does anyone?

To weather or not to weather? Most toy train hobbyists don't do it. No one's sure why. Some say it ruins the collector value. Others claim not to have the skill to do it well. Dick and John have repainted and lettered some poor-condition trains (ATSF at right rear), but there's something about a nice, glossy toy-train finish (Frisco in front) that keeps them from messing it up. If you don't have that hesitancy, go for it, as Kent Johnson did with this locomotive (CP Rail at left rear). It looks great and fits in with his "scale hi-rail" toy train layout.

- I don't worry much about the "investment" value of my trains, although at some point I would hope my wife or children will get *something* out of them beyond enjoyment.
- Yes, our layout would look better with weathered equipment. But "better" is a relative term. The layout we have is unabashedly a toy train layout. If I wanted a scale layout, I'd start by removing the center rail . . . nah!
- John and I are toward the operator end of the collector/operator group, so I could weather a few things, but on a layout I think it has to be all or nothing. A bright, shiny locomotive pulling weathered cars would look goofy.
- Yes, I'm skilled enough at weathering so the trains wouldn't look bad.
- Finally, I'm a nostalgic sap. No way I'm gonna weather my original 675 or my childhood red-stripe passenger cars. But that's just me. And John? Well, he'll repaint beaters to make them look new, but I've never seen any weathering—other than dust—on his trains.

So, that's why we've chosen not to weather our trains. But don't let us influence your decision.—*Dick Christianson*

Rolling stock resources

Greenberg's Guide to Lionel Trains, 1901-1942, Vol. 2: O and OO Gauges by Bruce Greenberg (10-7180)

Greenberg's Guide to Lionel Trains, 1945-1969, Vol. 1: Motive Power and Rolling Stock by Paul Ambrose (10-8195)

Greenberg's Guide to Lionel Trains, 1987-1995: Motive Power and Rolling Stock by Michael Solly (10-8285)

Greenberg's Guide to M.T.H. Electric Trains by Dick Christianson (10-8155)

Here's a tip that will improve the performance of some of your locomotives, especially those with short wheelbases. Run a jumper wire from the tender roller to the locomotive, effectively lengthening the locomotive. This eliminated stalling on the Atlas switches in the area of the passenger terminal.

In the end, it'll all come down to you picking what you like and what looks good.

answers reader questions in *Classic Toy Trains* magazine, switches seem to be a constant source of compatibility problems. Generally, manufacturers produce switches that work well with their own products and seem to ignore the rest. But even that hasn't always been a hard and fast rule. For example, there was a time when Lionel four-wheel-drive O-27 locomotives weren't compatible with the company's own O gauge switches.

The three recurring trouble areas with switches are derailments, short circuits, and temporary interruption of third-rail power. We dealt with two of them on the LL/SF.

After Dick and I had installed the Atlas switches in the passenger terminal, we found that almost all of our Lionel steam locomotives would lose third-rail contact momentarily when negotiating the turnouts at slow speed. It didn't happen with the diesels because their pickup rollers are spaced farther apart.

Since all the steamers have whistle tenders, the fix was quick and simple. We connected a supple black wire to the hot lug terminal on the side of the locomotive's E-unit, ran it back through the cab and into the tender. Then we hooked it to the leads coming from the whistle pickup rollers. This gave us third-rail continuity for the length of the locomotive and tender.

A common cause of short circuits has to do with objects or components hanging down too low as cars pass over the turnout. At best, it will create a big blue spark, at worst, a dead short. One night, Dick brought home a set of MTH near-scale-length heavyweight Pullmans—beautiful cars all—but as we sent them around the layout, about half of them sputtered and spit sparks as they crossed our Lionel O-72 switches.

Apparently, MTH's supplier had a quality-control problem. Some of the activator armatures on the couplers were hanging too low and hit the widened center rails at the frogs. The quickest remedy was to stick some black electrician's tape on the bottom of the offending armatures. When the tape comes off or wears out, we'll come up with a more professional fix.

There are no perfect worlds, not even the little ones we create to enhance the joy of running trains. Overcoming these challenges keeps the Yankee ingenuity flowing.

How do you make rolling stock "better"? Settle on a size, an era, a geographic region, a favorite prototype. Lots of ways to help your layout "make more sense." But in the end, it'll all come down to you picking what you like and what looks good to you.

9

Maintenance: Keeping the good times rolling

By John Grams

The best way any of us can improve our layouts—the step from which we'll derive the most satisfaction—is to make them run better. Whether you have a loop of O-27 gauge track and a tiny transformer or a gargantuan layout with everything command-controlled, if the trains don't run well, you might as well take up a different hobby.

What's involved in maintenance? How do you know when your trains need work? How often do you have to roll the locomotives into the engine shop?

Here's a familiar phrase: "The squeaky axle gets the grease." This adage probably goes back to the invention of the wheel. Unfortunately, by the time things start squeaking it may be too late. People tend to put things off until something breaks down, and that can be expensive.

Maintenance should be regular and preventative. Dick and I suggest that you set up a schedule – a rotation for regular service of everything on your layout – and stick to it. The time interval will depend on how much you run your trains, but we think that once a year should be the minimum. Lubricants dry out over time just sitting on a shelf.

> **Key maintenance questions**
>
> • If I build a really big layout, am I going to be able to keep it clean?
> • Can I reach all the track?
> • Will I be able to reach as far as I need to with a vacuum hose?
> • Will I affix everything so it can't be sucked up by the vacuum?
> • How often do I plan to run trains? What will that do to them in terms of maintenance?
> • Do I like to tinker with mechanical things? How about electronics?
> • Do I have access to a toy train hobby shop with a good service center?
> • Do I have access to a hobby shop that stocks ample toy train parts?

Postwar rolling stock should be put on a regular maintenance schedule.

Locomotives

Contemporary locomotives with can-style motors and electronic circuits for reversing, sound, control, and whatever else, are virtually maintenance free in the traditional sense. Of course, when problems arise, fixing them is no longer a job for the mechanically inclined backyard (or basement) mechanic. We're talking circuit boards, chips, memory cards, resistors, thermistors, gaflidgits, and weebkniffls! When the trains go into the shop, just like your automobile, very little gets fixed; most of it just gets replaced. That's the way it is with new things.

Of course, moving parts, such as gears and axles, should be lubed as needed, and wheel treads and pickup rollers should be kept clean, but that's about it. Because every locomotive is a bit different, it's wise to consult your owner's manual for particulars. These motors and circuit boards are amazingly reliable if not abused or misused and usually carry a warranty against defects.

The older engines with conventional AC/DC universal motors and mechanical reverse units require a lot more attention. In addition to routine cleaning of the wheel treads and pickup rollers, and lubricating the gears and axles, the motor requires periodic attention.

The armature shaft needs lubrication often. On some motors both ends are exposed, on others only one. Because just one drop of oil is recommended—any more may run down and foul the commutator—it has to be administered often or the bearings will wear out. Some motors have an oil wick that holds two or three drops, so needed lubrication can be less frequent.

The commutator face must be kept clean and the slots free of debris. On many locomotives this is possible without taking the motor apart by using a cotton swab dipped in mineral spirits on the face and a wooden toothpick in the slots. Brush holders can sometimes be flushed clean with a few drops of mineral spirits. TV tuner cleaner in a spray can and clean cotton swabs can be used instead of the mineral spirits, but this can be expensive. Your local Radio Shack carries TV tuner cleaner.

Air whistle motors need the same kind of periodic attention—motor cleaning and armature shaft lubrication. However, the service interval can be longer because they aren't used as often.

Cars

Modern-era cars with fixed axles, fast-angle wheels, and needle-bearing trucks

Keeping track clean is a never-ending challenge. Dust from the air, combined with oil from motors, turns into a sticky, black sludge on car and locomotive wheels. A track-cleaning car can be helpful, especially in hard-to-reach areas, but it's not the ultimate solution.

This track-cleaning car (the idea comes from scale model railroading) is the authors' answer to dirt. It slides along with the car, wiping dust and residue as it goes. When it's time to clean the cleaner, Dick and John simply change the felt pad.

don't need much attention. Lubrication isn't necessary most of the time. If gunk (the technical term for that nameless hard black stuff) builds up on the wheels, it should be cleaned off. For some reason, that buildup doesn't happen as often as with postwar cars.

Postwar rolling stock should be put on a regular maintenance schedule, including cleaning the wheel treads with a solvent—sometimes they must be scraped off with a knife or screwdriver first. Then you need to lubricate each wheel (not tread) with one drop of oil. Spin it. If it doesn't revolve freely, use two drops.

Accessories

Accessories with regular electric motors are sometimes neglected because they aren't operated as often as locomotives. But they also need occasional service of the same kind as locomotives—keep them clean and lubricated. Accessory motors are more likely to be dealt with on an as-needed basis.

Accessories with vibration motors need tweaking if they aren't performing well. Otherwise, leave them alone. They tend to be flimsily constructed and easily damaged if prodded too often or in the wrong way.

Track

Track maintenance is vitally important to smooth operation. Ideally, all the track on a layout should get a deep cleaning several times a year—more often in sections that carry heavy traffic. This means applying elbow grease and a ScotchBrite pad until dirt, grime, and oxide are removed and the rails look bright.

Several liquid track cleaners were made specifically for this job. Some other household cleaning and degreasing products can be used on a regular basis between scourings. These are usually applied on a soft cloth that needs to be turned frequently.

Dick and I acquired a Centerline Products rail cleaner about the time we finished laying track. This patented device consists of a heavy casting on two coupler-equipped trucks. It has a rectangular open space in the center to place a cylindrical, absorbent, fabric-covered roller.

We saturated the roller with a cleaning and grime-removing liquid called "Goo-Gone." Next, we coupled the rig behind a locomotive and ran it around the layout a few times. The free-rolling roller deposits the Goo-Gone on the rails as it goes about the layout.

Although Dick and I found that the roller did loosen and pick up some grime from the railhead, much of it was left suspended in a film of Goo-Gone. Getting the rails really clean required a follow-up with a dry rag.

So Dick and I invented a wiper car, designed to finish the job by mopping up after the rail cleaner. We modified a home-

All the track on a layout should get a deep cleaning several times a year.

> ### Maintenance resources
>
> *Beginner's Guide to Repairing Lionel Trains* by Ray L. Plummer (10-8095)
>
> *Greenberg's Repair and Operating Manual for Lionel Trains, 1945-1969* (7th edition) by Roger Carp (10-8160)
>
> *Toy Train Repair Made Easy* by Ray L. Plummer (10-8250)

> ### Maintenance tips
>
> - Set up a regular schedule for maintenance of rolling stock and accessories.
> - Clean locomotive wheel treads and pickup rollers.
> - Lubricate locomotive gears and axles.
> - Oil motor armature-shaft bearings.
> - Swab the motor's commutator face with solvent.
> - Clean car wheel treads. What is that black gunk anyway?
> - Lubricate car wheels at the axles.
> - Don't neglect accessories with motors in them.
> - Keep track clean and bright at all times.

made track cleaner that model railroaders have used for years.

First, we cut a piece of 2 ¼" x 3" Masonite, beveled the 2 ¼" widths (from the bottom to the top edges) to keep them from catching on track joints or switches, and used epoxy to attach sawed-off nails to the Masonite. Then we drilled two holes in the bottom of a stockcar to match the position of the nails. We inserted the nails into the holes so that, as the stockcar rolls around the layout, it drags along the Masonite.

That's as far as two-rail model railroaders go. They use this device as a track polisher, removing the "sled" now and then and lightly sanding away the dirt.

Dick and I could have done that too, except for the "curse of the third rail"! The center rail is higher than the outer ones because of the fiber insulators under it. Using our device as-is meant that we'd polish only the center rail!

Our solution was to cut two 3" lengths of .032" (the thickness of the insulator) brass strip (styrene would also work) and use epoxy to glue them to the Masonite where they would ride on the outside rails.

Then we bought some inexpensive felt-like material at a sewing store and cut it to 2 ¼" x 4" pieces that we wrapped around the sled lengthwise. A rubber band close to each outside edge holds everything in place.

Voila! A track-wiping car. We couple it behind the rail cleaner, and the two units work together to do a job that's good enough to last between regular scouring with the ScotchBrite.

Overall layout cleaning

Eventually dust settles on every part of a layout, covering it with a blanket of dull gray. A little dust can provide an aura of realism—a dingy weathered look—but there comes a time when your figures are standing ankle deep in dust that resembles volcanic ash.

There is no easy recommended procedure for layout cleaning—it depends to a large extent on how securely you've fastened down everything. I've seen people go after the dust with everything from feather dusters and paintbrushes to shop vacs (put a woman's nylon over the nozzle so you don't suck up any Plasticville people). Perhaps the answer for you lies somewhere in between.

Unfortunately, this is everyone's least favorite part of the hobby. That's why this chapter's short! But it's an integral part of making your layout better, especially in terms of performance.

If you take time to clean and lube now and then by making it a regular part of your operating schedule (e.g., the first week of February and the first week of August), you'll have a lot more fun with your layout the other 50 weeks of the year!

10

Operation: A brave new toy train world

By Dick Christianson

If you're a typical toy train fan, you're probably asking, "What's a chapter on operation doing in a toy train book?" Or, "Operation? How do you operate trains on a loop?" Or, "What do you mean 'operation'? My trains run fine."

In scale model railroading circles, "operation" is the term for running trains realistically. It can include switch lists, car order cards, a fast clock, realistic speeds, guys communicating over headsets, dispatching, signaling, and post-operating-session critiques.

Other hobbyists just get a kick out of watching their trains go 'round and 'round in circles. And who's to say which of these approaches to model railroading is right and which is wrong? Not me. Not John.

So, let's start this chapter with this understanding: If you want to build a big loop of track around the basement walls and just watch the trains run, good for you. Go for it. They're your trains.

If, on the other hand, you want to build a layout that's fully scenicked, has lots of intricate trackwork, and is designed for realistic operation, that's fine too.

> **Key operating questions**
>
> • Can I imagine operating my toy trains on my toy train layout?
> • Can I imagine being bored because my layout has no operating possibilities?
> • Can I design my track plan to include operating possibilities?
> • How about accessories? Can I build some operation around them?
> • Will operation work better for me if I use command control?
> • Have I designed in power blocks?
> • How about remote-control uncoupling sections? Can I position them to enhance operation?
> • Do I realize that backing long trains through O-31 switches without derailing them is next to impossible?

The "big however"

However, if you've always run trains in circles and never "operated" them, you may be surprised at what you're missing. In fact, John and I agree that there's an inherent danger in not giving operation at least a half-hearted effort. When you start putting your track plan on paper, we recommend that you think through the routes your trains are going to run and how many people will be running the trains. Consider, too, whether you'll need to turn the trains by hand or include a reverse loop, whether you're going to include industries and pretend to deliver goods, where you're going to need to place your uncoupling sections, and where you'll put your control panels (if using conventional controls).

If you don't consider these questions, you run the risk of building a layout, running the trains around it for a month or so, and before a year is out being bored to tears and looking for a more exciting hobby (stamp collecting, scrapbooking?).

Appreciating operation

Let's talk about some generally underappreciated aspects of operating toy trains.

Historically, toy trains have been (and still

Lionel and Flyer, from their earliest beginnings, were built with operation in mind.

are) way ahead of scale models when it comes to operation. Most of us who are toy train fans haven't looked at the hobby this way, but it's true. Lionel and Flyer, from their earliest beginnings, were built with operation in mind. Consider these features: remote-controlled track switches, sound and smoke, and lights and signals. Don't forget operating accessories that included numerous industries and facilities—logging and lumber, coal, a variety of small operations like milk and cattle, locomotive servicing, and passenger and freight facilities.

With the exception of electrically operated switches, only in the past decade have scale models begun to include these features—and then only in their locomotives! Where are the HO scale dump cars, log loaders, and sawmills? The coal loaders, working water tanks, and transfer tables?

So why haven't we toy train guys taken advantage of this opportunity by embracing operation? That's a question I can't answer.

Use your imagination again

Let's say you're interested in the lumber industry and want to build a layout based on lumber. At one end of the layout you have a log loader. A Lionel Geep backs a string of

Here's an idea for an operating layout. Take an operating oil derrick or two, add some pipe made from conduit (metal or plastic), get a Lionel pipe loader, throw in some tank cars and gondolas or flatcars carrying pipe, move them from place to place, and you have a layout set in Oklahoma during the days of the oil boom. You can do similarly themed layouts using lumber, coal, and cattle.

empty log cars into a siding where logs are—automatically—loaded onto them.

When the log cars are filled, the Geep hauls them out of the siding (switches thrown remotely) and onto the main line. They're switched into an interchange track, uncoupled, and left until the local picks up the cut of log cars and takes it to the other end of the layout, where the cars are dumped at the Lionel sawmill.

You can run similar operations with cattle cars, tank cars, coal hoppers and loaders, or freights with merchandise cars and milk cars. Simple, but fun.

I'm sold. What's next?

Okay, so you're willing to work some operating possibilities into your layout design. As

> **Operation resources**
>
> *HO Lineside Industries You Can Build* (12168)
> *HO Trackside Structures You Can Build* (12143)
> *Model Railroader's Guide to Locomotive Servicing Terminals* by Marty McGuirk (12238)
> *Realistic Model Railroad Operation* by Tony Koester (12231)
> *Track Planning for Realistic Operation* (3rd edition) by John Armstrong (12148)

with almost every other chapter in this book, decisions you made earlier or other circumstances such as the shape of the room, space available, equipment you own, and available resources will play a role in the decisions you make regarding operation.

Operating toy trains doesn't require a huge layout. If you have only a 4 x 8, some simple operation is possible. Using a loop of O-27 track and a siding or two, you can design a layout with a theme. How about using tank cars, a couple of oil wells, plastic conduit cut to look like pipe, flatcars to carry the pipe, and a pipe-loading accessory?

Or think about the possibilities of an

Doodlebug operation on the LL/SF

I remember when Lionel came out with its Baltimore & Ohio Budd Rail Diesel Cars in the 1950s. We didn't have anything like those RDCs in northern Wisconsin where I grew up, and so I thought they looked weird. Didn't appeal to me at all. Eventually, I came to appreciate those models more, and today I think they're pretty neat. However, what I really like along those lines are doodlebugs.

So, when MTH came out with its Santa Fe doodlebug a couple years ago, I bought one. That model looks great and runs smoothly on the LL/SF. Now that the layout is fully operational, the doodlebug has been presented with a new world of operating possibilities.

Although you may not have a doodlebug, you should consider applying an operation similar to what I'm about to describe using RDCs or another mixed-consist train.

The passenger yard ladder leads onto the main line.

Depending on which direction I want to work in, the doodlebug heads out or backs out onto the main.

This morning the doodlebug has in tow an MTH combine—a little extra freight and some additional passengers to pick up on the other side of the freight yard. Most of the passengers are workers at the oil field on the other side of the layout; others are businessmen who work in a nearby suburb.

Leaving the passenger terminal, the doodlebug heads onto the main line. After crossing the river on the vintage yet serviceable bascule bridge (it only smokes a little now and then), the train rolls to a stop. The engineer backs the consist over the bridge and into the siding to pick up the fully loaded Lionel milk car.

Once that's coupled up, the bug heads across the river again. It rumbles through a couple of grade crossings, passes the wye track leading to the engine-servicing terminal, and eventually reaches the freight yard.

At this point the train needs to make a couple back-and-forth moves through the freight ladder to reach the yard lead. The little train backs down the lead until the yellow caution light goes on in the yard tower (an operator's signal to the yard lead passes through the backdrop and is hidden). Getting clearance from the tower, the engineer throws her into forward and heads onto the branch line leading to the oil field. The train rattles along the poorly maintained branch

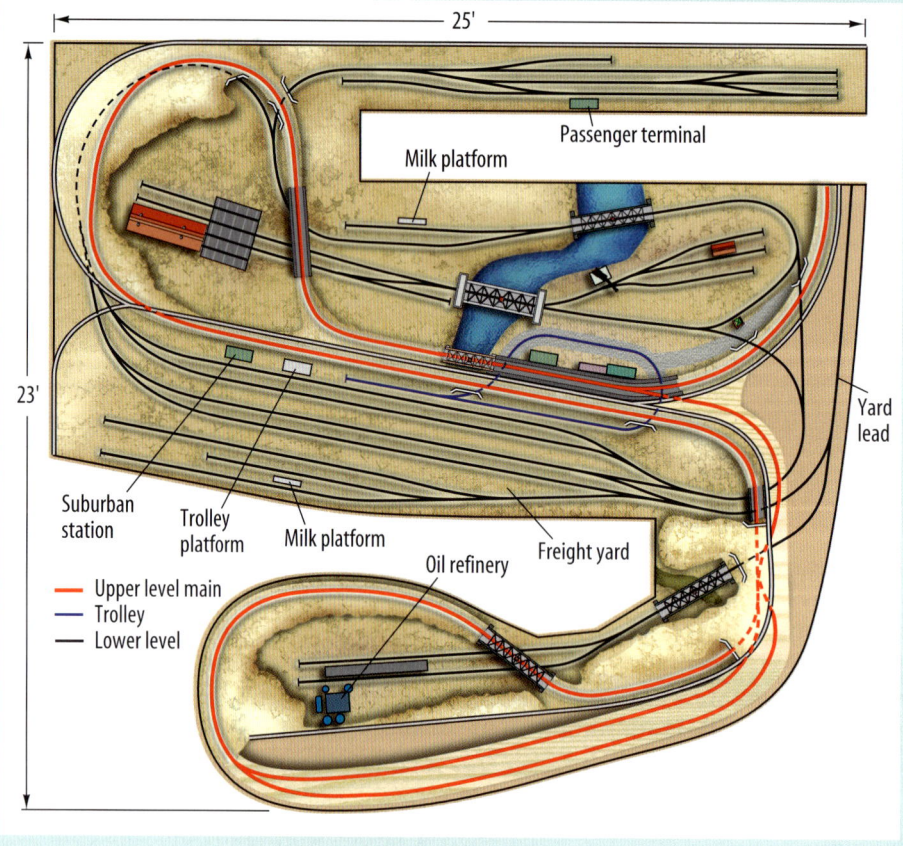

line (some of the track has been around for more than 50 years!), passing under the Santa Fe's high-speed main line and over the old but freshly painted Marx through-truss Trouble Water bridge. In only a few moments, the little consist pulls into the storage tracks at the oil field.

It doesn't take long for the workers to disembark and unload a few pieces of drilling equipment. Soon, the engineer eases the doodlebug into reverse and backs out of the yard, rolls across the river, and backs onto the freight yard lead.

When given the all-clear, the engineer puts the throttle in forward, and the little bug rocks and rolls down the siding. This time, instead of zigzagging through the yard ladder, the engineer continues down the siding to the milk platform near the barrel loader ramp.

Once she comes to a stop, the bug's remaining passengers can disembark here as well, but they have to cross seven tracks to get to the passenger and trolley stations as well as the business district on the other side of the tracks. So, if they haven't finished the morning paper, they can stay on the train until the engineer backs onto the yard lead, the tower operator throws a switch, and the train heads for the other end of the yard.

At the far end of the yard, the tower operator throws the switch, and the bug's engineer backs his train to the suburban station where the rest of his charges get off. A half-dozen or so businessmen board the train here for a ride to the passenger yard to catch the mid-morning-departing Super Chief.

The engineer doesn't have to back down too far to get to the wye. The yardmaster throws the switch and the bug—milk car first—backs into the engine terminal track. Once he's cleared the end of the wye, the tower operator throws the switches and the doodlebug returns to the main, head end first, for the short trip to the station.

The engineer's morning responsibilities are almost done, but not until he has returned the milk car to the dairy siding. There's still some time before the Super Chief departs, so the yardmaster gives the engineer clearance, and he backs out of the terminal and onto the main line. The empty doodlebug has to make the run across the river and into the wye again, where the entire train is turned and backed down the main to the siding.

Once the milk car has been uncoupled, the doodlebug and combine pull ahead onto the main, cross the bridge, and return once again to the terminal. Quite a morning's work for a little train. Enough to keep me busy and out of trouble for 10 to 15 minutes.

Hmmm, maybe there's something to this scale operation business.—*Dick Christianson*

Early morning on the LL/SF and the doodlebug and combine are ready to leave the station with a few passengers for the oil terminal and suburban station. There's a scheduled stop at the milk platform to pick up the local farmer's "white gold."

On the far side of the layout, the bug and its trailing cars have stopped across the freight yard from the suburban station. After it has unloaded the milk, it'll back down the siding, run to the end of the yard, and head back to the station. From there the train will head for the wye in the engine-servicing facility and turn around for home.

around-the-walls layout. You may want to treat it as though it were a point-to-point layout—the ultimate in model railroading realism! Trains start in a yard along the walls at the far end of the basement. A local freight heads out early in the morning with a variety of loads to deliver at sidings (with operating accessories) along the way.

First stop is the milk-loading platform. While it was yet dark, a local farmer delivered six or seven cans full of "Bessie's best" for pickup. With the milk car loaded, the train pulls out of the siding and back onto the main line. Next stop is the operating freight station where the merchandise car fires some boxes onto (or across!) the platform. Back on the main, the block signal indicates that the local needs to take the siding because the overnight express train is due to arrive from the opposite direction.

Once the Flyer has passed, switches are thrown for the main line and the local continues on its way. Next stop, the cattle loader, where seven cows are unloaded for pickup by a local rancher. The freight then stops at the station to pick up orders as well as top off its water. Don't forget the cans of milk. The dairy has a truck waiting at the siding to pick up the fruits of Bessie's labor.

This kind of layout suggests that you've already made a big decision. To get the most out of this operation, you're going to want to have walkaround control: TMCC or DCS (the Lionel and MTH systems) so you can follow trains around the basement.

Gauntlet hits the ground

Years ago, a toy train magazine author unintentionally issued a challenge to me when he noted that he had never seen a realistic freight yard operation on a toy train layout. As I read that, I heard the "thunk" of his gauntlet landing at my feet.

Construction of our layout was already under way, but John had repeatedly recommended ("demanded" is closer to the truth) that we add tracks to one side of the layout. Sensing the opportunity to prove that author wrong, I relented. "Okay," I said, "let's add a freight yard." And we did.

The layout John and I built, shown in the track plan on page 78, occupies maybe about one-third of the basement (about 23 x 25 feet) in our ranch-style home. It includes a long four-track stub-ended passenger yard with a switcher pocket and crossovers for engine runarounds; a mainline loop; a wye for turning locomotives (and some full-length trains) and leading trains to the engine-servicing facility (coal, water, sand, transfer table, enginehouse, and rip tracks). Off the same tracks we have sidings for coal and logging accessories.

On the other side of the layout, John and I have a long passing siding in front of the suburban passenger station. In the foreground, we have two more double-ended yard tracks. From both of them, a switcher can work its way to the front of the layout and the three stub-end yard tracks.

Off yard track no. 1 is a long lead that the yard switcher uses to make and break up freight trains. Off the yard lead, a locomotive works the local oil industry (two tracks). And that's just the lower level.

In terms of operation, the layout includes both passenger and freight operation. It has steam- and diesel-servicing facilities, along with industries where we can make deliveries and pickups.

How about operation? Because of the way John and I designed the layout, we can do timetable operation. We can operate with radios, switch lists, and a fast clock.

Do we? No. We'll be up front here. Sometimes we just start the trains running on the upper and lower loops and let them run.

Usually, though, when John and I operate the layout, here's what we do. John takes one side, and I take the other. I'll run passenger trains out of the yard and send them out around the main line for several trips. Then I'll return them to the yard. Maybe I'll cut off the locomotive, run it out onto the main to the wye leading to the servicing facility, and pull it up to the sanding tower and diesel-fueling accessory.

When that's done, I'll run the locomotive

back through the wye and return to the passenger yard. Then I'll run out another passenger train or maybe the doodlebug, trailing the milk car behind it.

On the other side of the layout, John is working the freight yard, making up a local or putting together a string of cattle cars. He enjoys running the switcher down the yard lead, throwing the switch, and backing across the river to the oil terminal to pick up a string of tank cars.

What John and I do is relaxed and unstructured, but it is operation. And it definitely beats watching trains go 'round and 'round and 'round.

Here's our recommendation. When you design your layout—soon now!—include opportunities for some level of operation, even if it's just a couple of sidings with accessories along them. It will give you something to do after the track is laid, the wiring's done, and the scenery is finished. It will delay the question, "Is that all there is?"

Let the journey begin!

Did you note that I said "delay" the question? At some point, no matter how big and complex and beautiful and interesting your layout is, you will ask, "Is that it?" You will look for more challenges and a change of scenery.

Nothing wrong with any of this. That's what this hobby is all about. It's why we wrote this book. We know that all over the country, toy train fans are ready to build their next layout. Our hope is that the suggestions we've made here, the questions we've asked, and the tips we've offered will make your next layout "better."

Good luck and enjoy building *your* better toy train layout.

Operating tips

- Design the use of accessories such as the coal loader, log loader, water tower, and so forth into your layout operation.
- Try to include O-72 minimum switches off the main line.
- Reserve O-31 switches for spurs and industrial sidings where you'll be backing only a switcher and three or four cars.
- Recognize that you can operate toy trains as well as, if not better than, you can operate scale trains. They were designed to be operated.
- Consider running unit trains: stockcars from Kansas through the Southwest to Los Angeles, coal hoppers through the Appalachians, tank cars from Texas and Oklahoma to the East Coast, log cars from the Pacific Northwest.
- Give your layout a name and create a purpose for its existence.
- Put a locomotive-servicing facility on your layout to service locomotives after they come off the main line.
- Design in enough aisle space for more than yourself. If you operate you may need room for two, three, four, or more people.
- If operation appeals to you, consider using command control with walkaround throttles.

Suppliers

Arttista
105 Woodring Lane
Newark, DE 19702
Highly detailed figures

Atlas "O"
378 Florence Ave.
Hillside, NJ 07205
Detailed engines, cars, track, and accessories

Bachmann Plasticville Buildings
1400 E. Erie Ave.
Philadelphia, PA 19124
Plastic kits for your layout

Bowser
P.O. Box 322
Montoursville, PA 17754
Detail parts and accessories

Classic Toy Trains Magazine
21027 Crossroads Circle
Waukesha, WI 53187
Top-rated toy train magazine

Die Cast Direct
1009 Twilight Terrace
Frankfort, KY 40601
Model cars, trucks, and figures

GarGraves Trackage
8967 Ridge Rd.
North Rose, NY 14516
Flexible track and switches

Greenberg Train Shows
P.O. Box 1192
Lombard, IL 60148
Train shows and auctions for collectors and operators

K-Line Products
P.O. Box 2831
Chapel Hill, NC 27515
O Gauge engines, cars, and accessories

Lionel Electric Trains
50625 Richard West Blvd.
Chesterfield, MI 48051
Premier manufacturer of modern-day electric trains

Marx Trains
358 W. Army Trail Rd, #140-338
Bloomingdale, IL 60108
Metal-lithographed trains

MTH Electric Trains
7020 Columbia Gateway Dr.
Columbia, MD 21046
Wide assortment of O gauge trains and accessories

Scenic Express
1001 Lowry Ave.
Jeannette, PA 15644
Everything scenic for your model railroad

Train Collectors Association
P.O. Box 248
Strasburg, PA 17579
Collector association for all vintage or modern electric trains

Trains Magazine
21027 Crossroads Circle
Waukesha, WI 53187
Great source for real-life train magazines and books

Third Rail Products
37 S. Fourth St.
Campbell, CA 95008
Manufacturer of detailed brass locomotives and rolling stock

Walthers, Inc.
5601 W. Florist Ave.
Milwaukee, WI 53218
Detail parts for O gauge railroaders

Weaver Models
P.O. Box 231
Northumberland, PA 17857
Detailed O gauge locomotives, cars, and accessories

Williams Electric Trains
8835-F Columbia-100 Pkwy.
Columbia, MD 21045
Traditional electric trains

Woodland Scenics
P.O. Box 98
Linn Creek, MO 65052
Scenery products for all gauges